I0159925

CHINESE CAMP

CAMP

The Haunting History of California's Forgotten Boomtown

Stephen H. Provost

STEPHEN H. PROVOST

All material © 2024, 2025 Stephen H. Provost
Cover concept and design: Stephen H. Provost
Cover photographs: Stephen H. Provost
All contemporary photos © 2024, 2025 Stephen H. Provost
Historical images are in the public domain, except where
noted.

Dragon Crown Books 2024
All rights reserved.

ISBN: 978-1-949971-48-4

Contents

Acknowledgments

My deepest thanks to Sharon Marie Provost for her assistance in laying the groundwork for this volume, both on site and in background research. I am grateful to Richard Beale of the Chinese Camp Store for allowing me to access to his extensive collection of historical photos and artifacts, and for his permission to share them here. Thanks also to Brad Fisher of the Tuolumne County Historical Society for his help in locating and permission to use several historical photos included here, and to veteran paranormal investigator Paul Dale Roberts for his insight into paranormal activity in Chinese Camp. In addition, I wish to acknowledge the valuable and extensive information included in two earlier works: Anne Bloomfield's 1994 book, *History of Chinese Camp Cultural Resources Inventory* (which, unfortunately, is no longer in print), and *The Big Oak Flat Road*, a 1955 volume by Irene D. Paden and Margaret E. Schlictmann, which focuses on freighting from Stockton to the Yosemite Valley.

Sharon Marie Provost in Solinsky Alley. *Author photo*

Foreword

One day, I was watching an early morning newsmagazine show that featured a story about a small gold rush town in California named Chinese Camp. I found the history of the place fascinating, and the visuals of the nearly abandoned town were stunning. Then and there, I vowed to one day visit this ghost town. Life happened and time got away from me, but it always sat there in the back of my mind.

Fast forward over a decade and I married an author of, primarily, nonfiction books with a love of history that matched or even surpassed my own. We spent our first two years together researching various highways around Nevada (our state of residence) and California, including the Lincoln Highway in Nevada and California, the Victory and Bonanza Highways in Nevada, and the Sierra Highway through Nevada and California.

Having been born in Sacramento, where I spent several years before moving to Nevada, I am extremely familiar with the Sierra Gold Rush towns along California's Highway 49. I had mentioned this historic road to Stephen and started researching some of those towns for a potential future research trip and book.

One weekend just before spring, we were restless and decided to take a Sunday drive along the northernmost section of 49—an area I was unfamiliar with. We were stunned at the absolute beauty and sheer volume of interesting historical sites between Vinton, California and Nevada City. That was all it took to inspire him (picture obsession) to start scheduling long weekend road trips for us.

When I began researching locations on the highway in preparation for these trips, what city should reappear to haunt me but Chinese Camp. I had never lost my desire to visit this historic ghost town, but I had forgotten exactly where it was located. Imagine my excitement when I realized this long-held desire was about to be fulfilled.

We left Carson City on a four-day road trip down the southern part of Highway 49 to its terminus in Oakhurst, in conjunction with a visit to the Calaveras Celtic Faire in Angels Camp. We didn't visit or document nearly as many cities as we had planned because of the overwhelming number of interesting places we found to investigate along the way. As we researched towns, we discovered many intriguing short detours off 49 to sites that were inextricably tied to these other mining boomtowns.

We finally got to stop at Chinese Camp on our last day as we headed home, only about an hour and a half before sunset. This wonderful ghost town was everything I had hoped for and so much more. The stormy weather was typical for early spring. The gloomy skies cast the perfect light for photography, creating just the right ambiance for a town that time seems to have forgotten.

But the town hasn't forgotten the bustling, important commercial hub it once was. The air was eerie and electric, not only from the storm, but from the very essence of the town itself.

We spent every moment of daylight we had left exploring the area and photographing the various buildings still standing, in differing stages of ruin. The only sounds disturbing the utter silence were the startling, spooky, woman-like screams of the wild peacocks that still inhabit the area. I am a horror writer myself, so the sense of life beating just under the surface and the otherworldly photographs I took inspired me to write a short story set in Chinese Camp ("Solinsky Alley," published in my collection, *Shadow's Gate*). I am profoundly grateful that I was finally able to visit this majestic boomtown and that my husband, Stephen H. Provost, is documenting the history of it.

I think you will enjoy this virtual visit to Chinese Camp, and maybe it will inspire you to go see this little slice of history before it crumbles to the ground.

Sharon Marie Provost

May 27, 2024

Note on the fire of 2025: We were heartbroken to learn that the Main Street structures shown in this book were gutted or leveled by the 6-5 Fire that swept through Tuolumne County in the first week of September 2025. This edition has been updated with an addendum to reflect this tragic event's consequences to the community and its history.

Stephen H. Provost

September 15, 2025

Looking north in 2024 from Solinsky Alley at the Cohn-Morris Store, which also served as the post office for many years. *Author photo*

CHINESE CAMP

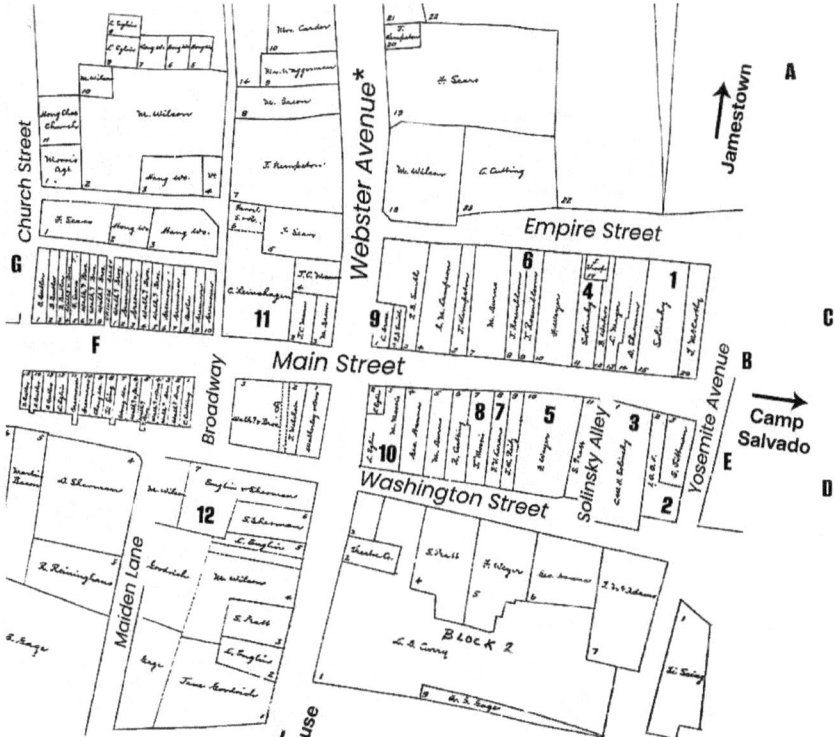

A. City Cemetery
B. Stratton Home (site)
C. St. Xavier's Church/Cemetery
D. Old Chinese Camp School (site)
E. IOOF Cemetery
F. Chinatown
G. Chinese Garden, churches (site)

* Webster Ave. = Red Hills Road

1. Cohn-Morris Store/Post Office
2. IOOF
3. Garrett House (site)
4. Fox Boarding House
5. Weyer Brewery (site)
6. New York/Rosenbloom Store
7. Frank's Fandango House (site)
8. Robert Orford Store
9. Gross Saloon
10. Morris Duplex
11. Saul Morris Home (site)
12. Louis Egling Wagon Shop and Blacksmith

1873

Map courtesy of Tuolumne County Historical Society,
adapted by the author

9

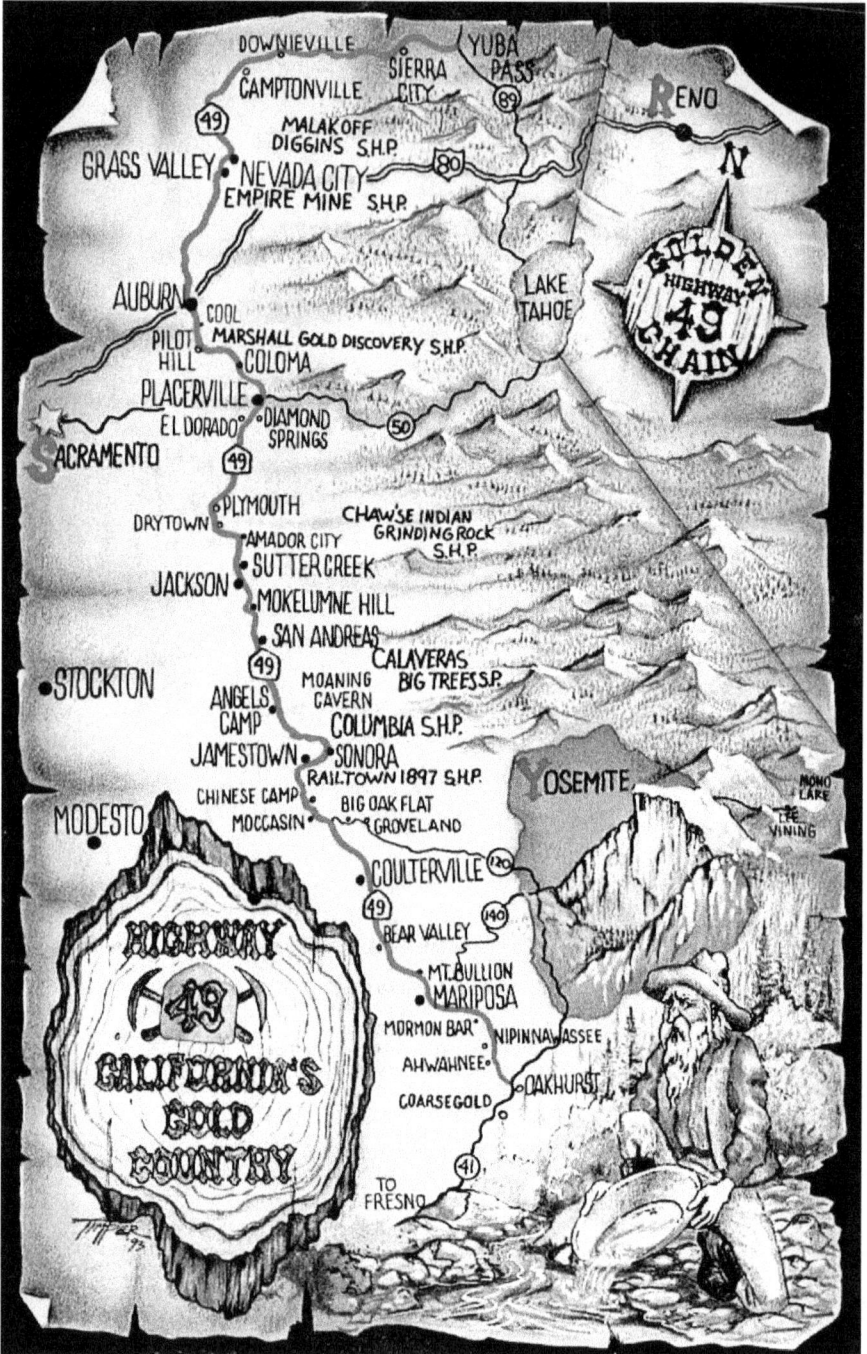

Vintage postcard shows the route of Highway 49 through Gold Country in California. *Author collection*

Looking east on Main Street toward State Route 49 in 2024, past the Robert Orford store, foreground right. *Author photo*

2024

Twilight came as we arrived in town... or maybe it had been there all along. Twilight seems to be the natural state of places like this one: Shadows cling to ghost towns with a tenacity they never display in cities full of life.

The towns are, if the truth be known, shadows of their former selves, so what else would any reasonable soul expect? Frozen in a state of eternal decay, hanging on to dreams long since denied, they whisper names forgotten by all those save the descendants of those who once dwelt there—if even they still remember.

But the whispers remain, drifting along on gentle breezes that rustle the leaves of the ailanthus trees brought from across the sea that reign supreme now. Their roots claw their way beneath and between the crumbling stonework, winding in and through the rotting wooden boards, obscuring what was and claiming it as their own.

Those who planted these trees are long gone from this place. "Celestials," men called them back then, because they came from a place whose emperor styled himself the "Son of Heaven." And these ailanthus, which they planted, were fittingly dubbed "trees of heaven."

If these trees could talk, what would they say? Do they miss the ones who planted them here? Do they yearn for a time when this town was alive with the sounds of horses' hooves and stagecoach wheels, of excited shouts at the discovery of gold in Six Bit Gulch, of men drinking and gambling and arguing? Or are they at peace, finally, now that they have the place to themselves?

The last of the "Celestials" departed a century ago now. They numbered in the thousands once upon a time; they lived and died and were buried here. But now even their remains are gone. The Celestials had a graveyard here once, but their descendants exhumed their bones, cleaned them, and returned them to their homeland. An eerie eyewitness account by longtime resident Helen Stratton tells how the bodies were removed every two years. Chinese priests and their assistants would come from San Francisco to exhume the remains, clean the bones thoroughly, and place them in small boxes for the trip back across the sea.

Those bones are gone. Now, only the trees remain, and those breezes that carry the echoes of what once was—stories told less and less often as time passes, but which, once you've heard them, rattle around in your head long after they've been shared by a dying campfire.

There are no campfires in this ghost town today, though the

word "Camp" is still part of its name. A few people still live here, in mobile homes, trailers, and scattered houses, but the population is itself a shadow of what it once was: fewer than a hundred when compared with several thousand in the 1850s. For every occupied dwelling, still more sit empty and abandoned, weathered and forgotten.

Elizabeth Fox took in boarders at the two-story house on Main Street once, but in 2024, it was barely standing collection of rickety boards, appearing like nothing so much as a haunted house from a Hollywood set. Joseph Rosenbloom sold mining supplies and dishes and tobacco at the New York Store, but the side have walls collapsed and the ceiling has caved in, leaving passers-by to mock its sturdy steel doors—once stalwart barriers against fire and theft and wayward cattle. Now useless.

And the Oddfellows Hall on the corner, the town's sturdiest structure, hasn't served its intended function for more than a century. Converted into a private residence, it stood vacant, conquered like so much else in town by the trees of heaven, before being gutted by the 2025 inferno.

Chinese Camp isn't heaven, though. Its seemingly perpetual twilight resembles nothing so much as a purgatory of a place stuck between past and present, a haven for ghosts and fading memories. Most of the old buildings on the abandoned Main Street carry "no trespassing" signs, which the visitor can't help but wonder at: Are they meant for the protection of these old, decaying properties, or as warnings to visitors that their own best interests are served by staying away?

Another warning, perhaps, is a sound that drowns out those whispers on the wind: the panicked, terrified shrieking of a woman in extreme distress. Being assaulted perhaps, or robbed. Or perhaps fleeing one of the many fires that plagued this and so many other Old West towns. Yet no women are to be seen on the street. Is it a ghost? A demon? Surely too loud to have been imagined... Then you see it there on the side of the road, a blue and green, almost fluorescent something, scurrying away from you.

Peacocks. They live here too now, adding some vibrant color to a largely gloomy place, proof that the living and the dead can live in peace with one another, much as the European and Chinese miners lived at (relative) peace with one another at the dawn of California's modern history, when the fever of gold drew men from east and west to what would soon become an important junction of wagon roads.

Sonora was the Queen of the Southern Mines. Columbia was the Gem of the Southern Mines. And Angels Camp was the Heart of the Southern Mines. This place carries no such epithet, but it surely deserves one: Perhaps "Crossroads of the Southern Mines" fits it best: a bustling Old West boomtown called Camp Washington at first, but shortly afterward, Chinese Camp.

Collectible ad from Charles Cutting's store in Chinese Camp. *Richard Beale collection*

Miners first found gold here in 1848 at Woods Crossing on Woods Creek, then founded Jamestown, just to the north. Chinese Camp is just a few miles south on Highway 49. *Author photo*

Making Camp

No one knows the exact date when Chinese Camp was founded. Like so much else about the town, that piece of information has been buried in the sands of history's hourglass.

What is known is that the Gold Rush of 1849 drew thousands of men (yes, overwhelmingly men) west to the Mother

Lode country that stretched from what's now Grass Valley and Nevada City in the north down through Sonora, to Coulterville and Mariposa—roughly along the path taken by modern California Highway 49.

There was, of course, no highway then: just old Native American trails that gave way to rutted wagon roads as fortune-hunters streamed into the soon-to-be 31st state. Over the course of two years, from 1850 to 1852, that state's population would nearly triple from fewer than 93,000 to 260,000. Many came overland, across the California Trail, which branched out across the Sierra as prospectors sought out unclaimed lands to mine and pan for gold. Some roads led to the Northern Mines on the more rugged slopes of the Sierra Nevada, while others made their way to the Southern Mines of what would become Tuolumne County and the nearby region.

But while European fortune-seekers came across the mountains from the east, other newcomers arrived by sea, crossing the Pacific from faraway China, a still-mysterious place sometimes called "Cathay" by Europeans. The first two Chinese immigrants arrived in San Francisco aboard the brig *Eagle* on February 2, 1848, and two years later 600 Chinese immigrants lived in California.

By 1852, however, that number had swelled to an estimated 25,000. Many came to work the railroads, but others sought their fortunes in the mines and surface diggings of the region.

Up the Creek

The first gold strike in Tuolumne came early in the summer of 1848 at Woods Creek, about a mile south of Jamestown. Shortly afterward, miners from Sonora, Mexico found more gold a little to the north—and named the camp they founded there for their home province.

Cattle at Woods Crossing in 1909.

The find near Jamestown caught the attention of four Englishmen who found themselves half a world away in Macau, on the southeast coast of China. According to a newspaper dispatch out of Stockton, they procured a vessel there built by Portuguese shipwrights that was described as an odd hybrid of a Chinese junk and a Portuguese schooner. It cost them a pretty penny—$20,000 to be precise—to get the ship ready, and still more to secure workers for their planned endeavor: They provided bonds to thirty-five Chinese workers to guarantee their wages for two years' worth of work in the mines once they arrived in California.

At first, everything seemed to be going as planned for the Englishmen, who crossed the Pacific before navigating the San Joaquin Delta eastward to the inland port of Stockton. From there, they traveled to Woods Creek, arriving before the rainy season.

They settled on a spot a good distance south of the original find near Jamestown: a location described as a few miles northwest of the Tuolumne River. It was, in those early days, as much a gold *scramble* as a gold rush: a race to the next big strike. Tents were pitched, claims were staked, and digging commenced.

If gold wasn't promptly discovered (and sometimes, even if it was), stakes were pulled up, and it was on to the next promising claim.

It didn't make sense to settle for scraps at the original Jamestown site when you could explore new potentially rich goldfields downstream—which is exactly what the Englishmen appear to have done. Following Woods Creek south from Jamestown (roughly parallel to modern Highway 49), they continued until they found a promising claim a few miles northwest of the Tuolumne River.

There, they appear to have set up camp at a placed called Camp Salvado or Salvador. Perhaps the name was a nod to the Portuguese boatbuilders, São Salvador do Campo being a former civil parish in Portugal, or perhaps they found other miners already working in the area who had some connection to San Salvador. Whatever the origin of the name, a mining camp was established there, about a mile east of where Chinese Camp sits today.

The Englishmen set up a stone building at Camp Salvado and appeared to be on the brink of success when the Chinese men they had recruited abandoned them, either of their own volition or because they were chased out by new arrivals intent on staking their own claims in the area.

And plenty of new arrivals there were: In addition to white prospectors, hundreds of Mexicans poured into the area.

Whatever the reason for their departure, when the Chinese left Camp Salvado, the Englishmen who'd hired them had no one to do their mining... and no choice but to give up on their dream. According to an account in a Stockton newspaper, "they sold out, left the mines, and the entire enterprise proved a failure."

A New Yorker named E.W. Emory set up a mercantile in the stone building they had constructed, and John Reitz opened a saloon (described by a later writer as "a notorious fandango house hangout for Mexican bandits and other outlaws near Chinese

Camp").

In short order, Camp Salvado developed a reputation as a rough-and-tumble mining town where American, German, Mexican, and Chilean miners all competed for gold. One particular incident illustrates just how rough it could be: In 1855, the first Amador County sheriff, William A. Phoenix, arrived with his undersheriff to arrest a fugitive wanted for murder in the town of Rancheria.

They tracked the man to Reitz's saloon, where a struggle ensued, and the sheriff—distracted by the danger posed to a bystander—missed his opportunity to subdue the wanted man.

He paid for it with his life, but the renegade was subsequently captured and hanged from a big oak tree south of the settlement.

Despite its reputation, it was not long before the gold ran out at Camp Salvado, and the miners moved on. The town was still active in 1861, when records show a couple named Lewis Shuman and Mary Shaloss were married there, but it eventually faded away into obscurity, and nothing is left of it today.

The Chinese Foundation

The Chinese, meanwhile, moved on to better fortune. But they didn't have far to travel: They settled just a mile to the west, on the other side of Rocky Hill, where they found another group of miners prospecting at a place called Camp Washington.

Here they received a warmer welcome, and it wasn't long before the word spread and other Chinese immigrants began to join them there. Some came down from Sonora and other large frontier towns, where authorities were enforcing a new $20-a-month tax on foreign miners passed by the California legislature in 1850. "Foreign," in this case, was shorthand for Chinese and Latin American miners, as the tax was seldom enforced on Europeans. (It caused an outcry that led to its repeal, although it

Chinese workers with flour sacks in the late 19th century. *Photo courtesy of Richard Beale, Chinese Camp Store*

was eventually reinstated as a license fee at a much lower rate of $4 a month.)

A few Chinese on the frontier was one thing. A cook named Ah Chi was celebrated when he began serving grizzly bear steak and wild pigeon pie at his makeshift shack on Washington Street in Sonora. He cooked it all on a piece of sheet iron over river rock and served it up on a pine table. But when more Chinese started arriving—and hunting for a share of the gold—the forty-niners were none too pleased with the competition.

On a single day, February 25 of 1853, a group of 200 Chinese found their way to the Southern Mines from the San Joaquin Valley.

The number of Chinese residents soon spiked into the thousands, and their influence was such that Camp Washington soon became known as Chinese—or sometimes Chinee—Camp, or Chinese Diggings. The original name isn't found in many places, but it is preserved in one of the two main east-west streets through town: Washington Street.

Before long, four of the Chinese "Six Companies" had a presence in the town. These Six Companies, each representing a district or clan, had joined forces in San Francisco to protect the interests of Chinese immigrants during the Gold Rush. Operating collectively as the Chinese Consolidated Benevolent Association, they helped Chinese Americans find jobs, housing, and food.

But other newcomers were arriving, too, with 168 white men counted living there in April of 1850. In addition to the miners, who made up most of the population, six merchants had set up shop there, along with three farmers, two teamsters, and a doctor with the surname Erwin.

Some of them were Irish, refugees from the potato famine, who made up a large number of the European population in Chinese Camp (hence the Catholic Church on the hill). But there were Germans, ethnic Jews, Poles, and others as well.

Then there were the Spanish-speaking miners: Mexicans and other Latin Americans who'd come up from the south, along with *Californios*—settlers who'd been there when the land had been part of Mexico. Some still regarded it as *their* land, and the forty-niners as invaders helping themselves to the gold that was rightfully theirs.

That some tension should exist among these groups was to be expected, especially considering the success being found by prospectors there. Nevertheless, the antipathy of the white settlers toward the Chinese was largely restrained in the Southern Mines—especially when compared with the animosity shown Chinese workers in other parts of the Mother Lode. The *Stockton Journal* would comment on this state of affairs in May of 1852:

This creek runs parallel to Sims Road just west of Chinese Camp. Miners had to haul their dirt to Sims Ranch to access the water needed to separate gold from their dry diggings. *Author photo*

"A friend who is working on Wood's creek, writes us that the diggings in that part of the Tuolumne co. continue to sustain their high reputation, and determined industry is well rewarded. An agitation is going on upon the subject of the Asiatic influx. There are some men who would like to carry out the harsh measures adopted in the northern mines; but our correspondent thinks there is too much humanity in Tuolumne county to allow any race of men to be oppressed, however desirable it may be to remove them. The creek, he says, is lined with Chinamen on both sides, from Jacksonville to Sonora, and harsh measures will only be resorted to for self-protection, in case the number of Asiatics increases."

As long as the Chinese kept to themselves and didn't go after the richer diggings, the forty-niners tended to leave them alone. And many Chinese seemed content to work areas that gave up a small bit of gold, using a method called "scratching."

Most of the precious metal was spread evenly near the surface of the landscape, so deep mines weren't needed. The problem lay when it came time to wash the gold, which was a major undertaking because there was no source of water in Chinese Camp itself. The dirt containing the ore had to be hauled a significant distance to a creek on Sims Ranch or even farther to Six Bit Gulch.

Pioneer Paul Morris, a longtime resident of Chinese Camp, said black miners who had been freed from slavery "made their way to the gold mines at Chinese Camp and paid as much as $75 a cart load for royalty to work the placers. They had to cart the dirt two-and-a-half miles to Six Bit Gulch to get water in which to wash the placers; thus the road from Byrne's Ferry reached Chinese Camp."

Some prospectors lacked the patience for this and quickly moved on to what they hoped would be easier diggings. But the Chinese were resolute and established themselves as willing to do the difficult work necessary to obtain a payoff. Sometimes, they'd take a blanket by four corners and deposit all the dirt in the middle, then flip it up into the air and watch the heavier bits fall back on the blanket while the rest was carried away by the wind. In this way, they used the wind to separate the gold from the dirt.

Alternatively, they'd do the difficult work of transporting it all to a gulch and washing it there. In fact, some of the other miners would actually pay the Chinese—the rate was $15 per cartload—to haul the dirt to one of the creeks and wash it for them.

Eventually, however, they began to build ditches that brought water in from Woods Creek.

Edna Bryan Buckbee described the diligence and patience of

the Chinese prospectors of that period:

"Daily, long lines of weary and patient Chinese, wearing wide flapping pants, and blue cotton tunics, jade bracelets on their wrists, across their necks a long pole from both ends of which a basket [was] suspended, plodded from the camps to the gulches hoping to make their 'pile.'

Miners use a blanket to winnow gold in this illustration from 1860. *Library of Congress*

"These miners with their pigtails carefully braided and rolled possessed a droll sense of humor, not always appreciated by the Americans. Not many Americans or Europeans took the trouble to learn their customs or manners; the few who did were amply rewarded, for the Chinese proved to be friendly and generous."

Chinese miners formed their own companies but, rather than paying a wage to employees, they used a profit-sharing model that offered both incentive and reward for success. This system impressed no less a businessman than Leland Stanford. A railroad tycoon, lawmaker, and a longtime shareholder in Wells Fargo, he

Praise for Chinese in the West

"They seldom think of resenting the vilest insults or the cruelest injuries. They are quiet, peaceable, tractable, free from drunkenness, and they are as industrious as the day is long.

"They are a kindly-disposed, well-meaning race, and are respected and well treated by the upper classes, all over the Pacific coast. No Californian gentleman or lady ever abuses or oppresses a Chinaman, under any circumstances, an explanation that seems to be much needed in the East. Only the scum of the population do it—they and their children; they, and, naturally and consistently, the policeman and politicians, likewise, for these are the dust-licking pimps and slaves of the scum, there as well as elsewhere in America."

Mark Twain, *Roughing It*, 1872

"As a class they are quiet, peaceable, patient, industrious and economical. Ready and apt to learn all the different kinds of work required in railroad building, they soon become as efficient as white laborers. More prudent and economical, they are contented with less wages."

Leland Stanford, 1865

is perhaps most famous today for having founded Stanford University in Palo Alto.

"We find them organized into societies for mutual aid and assistance," Stanford wrote in 1865, referring to the Six Companies. "These societies can count their numbers by thousands, are conducted by shrewd, intelligent business men who promptly advise their subordinates where employment can

Leland Stanford.

be found on most favorable terms.

"No system similar to slavery, serfdom or peonage prevails among these laborers. Their wages, which are always paid in coin each month, are divided among them by their agents who attend to their business according to the labor done by each person. These agents are generally American or Chinese merchants who furnish them their supplies of food, the value of which they deduct from their monthly pay."

Wild West Outpost

On the whole, prospects were good, and excitement certainly was high. Interest in the area was strong enough that, by September of 1850, the Reynolds and Company Express had started transportation service from Sonora to the Southern Mines—almost certainly including Chinese Camp.

Just a month earlier, Tuolumne County itself had been organized: subdivided into six "townships," with Chinese Camp in the same district as Jamestown, Woods Creek, and settlements at Curtisville, Green Springs, Mountain Inn, and Yorktown. (Many of these names will seem unfamiliar to the modern reader, although Curtisville and Green Springs both had post offices by 1853.)

With all this activity, it was decided that the time had come to draw up formal rules for prospecting in the area. Accordingly, the word went out that an assembly would be held on September 17 at which miners in the area should gather to set up a form of self-government.

It was, at the time, an innovative idea. While some 15 camps in Tuolumne County would call similar meetings to set up ground rules over the next few years, Chinese Camp was apparently the first to do so. Countywide rules would eventually be established, but not until 1858.

In Chinese Camp, the miners reached agreement on several matters. For one, they decided that the boundaries of all claims should be marked off by ditches of a specific size, so there would be less room for dispute over neighboring claims. Furthermore, although they allowed established claims to remain at their present size, they limited the size of any future claims to no more than 20 square feet. Finally, to ensure that the new rules were abided by, they elected Isaac Capps to serve as alcalde (mayor/magistrate) and S.E. Chamberlain as sheriff to adjudicate legal matters and keep the peace, respectively. Capps was to be paid $3 for each settlement he arbitrated and $1 a mile in travel expenses, while Chamberlain would be given $2 for each service rendered and $2 a mile for travel.

Apparently, neither one of them stuck around for long: Capps' name is never mentioned in any newspaper article of the time, nor did it appear in the *Miners and Business Men's Directory* published in 1856. Neither did Chamberlain's name, although he was still in the area in 1853, when he was assessed for owning $300 in personal property.

As a lawman, he was either ineffective or outmanned—or both. According to one account, holdups and robberies of the sluice boxes used to separate gold from gravel became an almost daily occurrence. The situation got so bad that the town folk eventually got together and formed a vigilante committee in the summer of 1852 to dispense their own brand of justice.

They got their chance to do just that in December of that year, when a trio of highwaymen held up a livery stable in broad daylight. The robbers were apprehended and locked up to await trial, but the vigilantes had a grimmer fate in mind for them. They waited for a prearranged signal—the solitary tap on the fire bell—before storming the place where the three were being held. Before the sheriff could intervene, the robbers were dragged out and, in short order, hanged for their transgression.

The show of force seems to have had the desired effect, because for one full year after that, not a single major crime was reported in the camp.

Bigotry and Banditry

The above account, reported nearly a century later in the *Sacramento Union*, is interesting because it mentions a jail where the highwaymen were supposedly held. But there's some question as to whether there even *was* a jail in Chinese Camp. Old iron lock-ups and adobe cells from the era survive in places like Columbia and Coulterville along Route 49, but there's no evidence of any such building today in Chinese Camp.

In fact, there's no evidence the town ever had its own courthouse or town hall. The justice of the peace for many years, Charles Cutting, was a merchant who conducted hearings inside his store.

Does that mean the highwaymen were actually jailed elsewhere (in Jamestown, perhaps)? Or was there, at one time, a small building that served as a jail cell in Chinese Camp, but which has been lost to history? This is the kind of question that arises time and again looking back on the history of ghost towns: intriguing gaps and discrepancies that leave a haze of mystery hanging in the air, just barely too thick to penetrate.

What isn't at issue is the fact that life could be dangerous. There was gold to be had, and if they couldn't mine it, there were those quite willing to steal it... and kill you for it, if necessary. A man named Charles Hout learned this lesson, much to his detriment, near Poverty Hill on the shortcut to Sonora northeast of town. It was there that three Mexican bandits unburdened him of the $500 he was carrying, stabbing him for good measure in the process. The wound was fatal, but it had not worked its full effect on him before some miners found him lying in the road and asked him what had happened. Before he expired, he managed to give them a description of the men who had assailed him.

An armed posse of 500 miners was formed, and they caught up to the bandits at La Grange, killing two of them; unfortunately, the third escaped with the money.

Such robberies were commonplace—and not just in Chinese Camp, but all across the region. Often, Chinese miners were the targets, and often, the bandits were Mexicans. Their thinking was simple: They were less likely to arouse the ire of white miners by stealing from the Chinese, and thereby avoid the vigilante justice of "Judge Lynch" that was likely to follow.

The Mexican bandits had learned that Chinese miners typically went to town to cash in their gold dust on Sundays, so they lay in wait for them along the road. Though they targeted the Chinese in particular, anyone who came down the road was fair game. As with Hout, they would simply kill their targets and leave them lying to bleed out in the middle of the road.

When vigilantes caught up to the bandits, they responded by tracking down the perpetrators and stringing them up on a hanging tree just north of Chinese Camp.

But vigilante justice, though swift and sure, wasn't always... well... *justice*.

One of the last Chinese residents of Chinese Camp, "China Mary," recalled an incident in the late 1850s in which three Mexicans overpowered the person tending the miners' ditch, Criss Gross. They wanted to keep Gross from interfering with their efforts to divert water from the ditch. A struggle ensued, and Gross shot one of the three assailants, wounding him, before he "died stretched out on a log," having been "literally hacked to pieces with dirk knives."

The man who had been wounded by Gross' gunshot was caught and confessed, and two other suspects were caught and brought before a mob in front of Paddy Burns' bakery. The shop's delivery wagon was brought up, and a rope was secured, whereupon the two men were tied to the back of it and dragged through the streets.

At an oak tree just outside of town, at the junction of roads leading to Montezuma and Chinese Station, they strung up the first of the nearly dead men. They were about to repeat the process with the second when James Morris, the shopkeeper, intervened. It's a good thing, too, because it was later discovered that the man hadn't taken part in Gross' murder after all.

The Murrieta Menace

In 1855, the *Jackson Sentinel* reported that "almost every Chinese camp in the northern part of this county has been robbed by gangs of armed Mexicans within the past few days. On Amador Creek alone, nine different camps had been plundered."

This was, however, nothing new.

Three years earlier, in January of 1852, a trio of Mexican bandits barged into Yaqui Camp—near the present hamlet of Calaveritas, just southeast of San Andreas. Word had apparently gotten out that a Chinese miner there had struck gold, and the bandits were intent on separating him from his profits.

The miner and his companions put up a fight, but the bandits managed to get away with $160 worth of gold dust.

In another robbery around the same time, a group of bandits attacked another group of Chinese miners, this time making off with two big bags full of gold. As in the Yaqui Camp robbery, three bandits were involved. Were they the same three outlaws or another group of Mexicans targeting Chinese miners? Either conclusion was possible, but the robberies continued,

The Costa Store in Calaveritas was constructed by Luigi Costa in 1852, the same year Joaquin Murrieta struck Yaqui Camp in the Calaveritas mining district. Murrieta was known to frequent the town's gambling halls and fandango houses. *Author photo*

compounded by horse thefts and murders.

A posse cornered a dozen south of San Andreas, wounding one of them. But the outlaws responded by riding to Yaqui Camp and shooting up the place, killing a white man there before moving on and killing two more Americans at a mill near Jamestown in the evening.

Suddenly, it wasn't just a matter of Chinese miners being robbed. Americans were being killed, which meant a whole new level of notoriety for the bandits. Calls began to go out to expel Mexican miners from the Mother Lode, but it wasn't long before they coalesced around a single name, belonging to the purported leader of the outlaws.

Joaquin.

Some people said his last name was Carillo. Others called him Murrieta. Over the course of time, five different "Joaquins" emerged as suspects. Or were they all the same man? A posse pursued one outlaw to Fiddletown, north of Jackson and east of Plymouth, where he reportedly jumped up on a table at a gambling hall and declared, "I am Joaquin!" before escaping.

The governor was alerted, and in the meantime, the robberies continued, with Chinese miners typically the targets. One group was separated from $1,000 near Dry Creek, and another was deprived of $6,000 near Big Bar on the Mokelumne River—where one of the miners was found shot through the neck. Between February 11 and 13, bandits killed five Chinese men, chased 50 more out of a camp, and stabbed a white man in the neck to take his mule.

Having wreaked most of their havoc in Calaveras County, the outlaws fled south through Tuolumne, and it's no surprise that some claim memories of seeing the mysterious Joaquin near Chinese Camp.

The sons of Chinese Camp's most renowned blacksmith, Louis Egling, and two of his helpers said a man claiming to be Murrieta showed up at the smithy with several mounted men more than once, demanding immediate service. In each instance, Egling complied, shoeing his horses and being paid handsomely for his trouble.

The son of another local, Robert Curtin, recounted the story of Murrieta lying in ambush beside the road and waylaying a freight hauler named Daniel Cloudman, who owned a ranch a couple of miles from Green Springs, then unhitching the best horse and riding away—but not before paying the hauler far more than the animal was worth.

Such stories appear odd considering the ruthless nature with which the bandits in Calaveras deprived their victims of gold, horses... and their lives. Paying handsomely for a smith's services and stopping to compensate a freight hauler for a stolen horse seem out of character, to say the least. Were local memories foggy, or had people begun using the name Murrieta in such cases as a form of cachet? Or was it really Murrieta, feeling generous after a successful robbery or gambling win?

With "five Joaquins" supposedly running around, anything is possible.

What is known is that a group of Mexican bandits headed farther south into Mariposa County, and that someone alleged to be Murrieta was eventually caught far to the south and west, near Coalinga. The man in question's head was separated from his body, and the brigandry of Joaquin Murrieta, if not much of the mystery surrounding him, was put to rest.

Black Bart

Joaquin Murrieta wasn't the only famed outlaw who allegedly turned up in Chinese Camp. Black Bart was said to have made an appearance or two as well.

Bart wasn't his real name. He was actually Charles Bolton or Bowles, and he owed at least some of his success to the fact that he didn't *look* like an outlaw. In fact, he appeared downright respectable, dressing like a high-society gentleman, complete with a bowler hat and long velvet-collared coat.

He didn't drink or smoke, but he evidently had a sweet tooth: Saul Morris remembered seeing him as a frequent visitor to his family's store in Chinese Camp while the stage was stopped to change horses, where he always passed the time by purchasing candy.

The dapper outlaw didn't ride up alongside a stagecoach but actually purchased a ticket, and no one was the wiser. Then "Bolton" disappeared, and "Bart" was suddenly there, wearing a pillowcase or flour sack with eyeholes cut out over his still-intact bowler.

Charles Bolton or Bowles, aka Black Bart.

Once, he apparently dropped a sawed-off shotgun somewhere near Chinese Camp during one of his holdups. A newspaper account printed in 1922 recalled the incident:

"Today, the tourist or traveler who goes to Sonora or to Yosemite National Park by way of the Big Oak Flat Road passes through the town of Chinese Camp in the heart of Bret Harte country. On the right-hand corner of the intersection as the traveler turns to climb the road into the mountains is situated an erstwhile saloon, now a pool hall."

There, the article stated, in the front of the building, a space had been reserved for various treasures from years gone by: such things as parts of wagons from caravans that didn't make it all the way across the mountains and a bear trap with the remains of a captured bear.

The aforementioned sawed-off shotgun was "by far the most highly prized relic" in the collection, the article stated.

Bolton was wielding a shotgun in 1875 when he robbed his first stage, a Wells Fargo coach heading from Sonora to Milton at Funk Hill, about four miles outside of Copperopolis. He left behind a piece of paper bearing a brief handwritten message in verse:

> I've labored long and hard for bread,
> For honor and for riches,
> But on my corns' too long you've tread,
> You fine-haired sons of bitches.

Black Bart's career would both begin and end at Funk Hill, where he struck again with his 28th robbery in 1883.

Robert Curtin, the son of a rancher who spent nearly a quarter-century driving a 16-mule team between Stockton and the Southern Mines, had his home at Cloudman, about eight miles southwest of Chinese Camp. He recalled seeing the outlaw there, pacing back and forth on the porch of the family home, which also served as a stage stop, while he waited for the coach to resume its journey.

Curtin also remembered the outlaw's last robbery—and the strategy employed by Wells Fargo to safeguard its strongbox that led to his undoing.

When they started running stages, the company kept cargo such as jewelry and important papers in a heavily padlocked wooden box, with an iron box reserved for bullion, gold dust, and mine payroll cash. When a coach was robbed, the boxes were tossed out, and the outlaws rode away with them.

But by the time Bolton executed his second robbery at Funk Hill, Wells Fargo had taken further steps to safeguard valuables by bolting the iron strongbox to the floor of the stage. Curtin, who knew the driver of the stage that day, recounted that the outlaw ordered him to unhitch the coach and drive the horses up the road. Bolton stayed behind to break the box open with a hammer.

Unfortunately for him, a young man returning from a hunting trip on the stage took a shot at the outlaw. The shot hit him in the hand and, in the process, he dropped a handkerchief (full of buckshot) with a soiled laundry tag. This was the clue investigators needed to identify their man.

Once apprehended, Bolton was convicted and sentenced to six years at San Quentin. He was released after four years for good behavior and seems to have left prison a reformed man. Black Bart was never implicated in another robbery—or any kind of crime—after that, and simply vanished, never to be heard from again.

Crime of Passion

Not all crime in Chinese Camp was perpetrated by famous bandits. As you might expect, there were drunken brawls, gambling disagreements, and plenty of disputes over mining claims.

There were also matters of the heart to contend with.

The murder of J.H. Smith took place in Columbia, in a drinking establishment and house of ill repute known as Martha's Saloon at the southwest corner of Main and Jackson—where the California Store is today. But the trouble all started in Chinese Camp a few weeks earlier.

That's where the proprietor of the saloon (Martha, of course) had met and become fond of a man named John Barclay, who had lived there since arriving from New York in 1850 and was described as "a man of some means" who "owned a good claim" in the area.

Martha Carlos, a 22- or 23-year-old woman from Kentucky, had a less savory reputation. She wasn't just a saloon owner, but a madam and a prostitute, with the latter actually appearing as her stated profession in the 1860 census. She'd left her saloon in Columbia and may have relocated briefly to Chinese Camp with some of her fandango girls.

Despite her profession, Barclay took a shine to Martha, and they soon married, leaving Chinese Camp and returning to Columbia, where they reopened her saloon—which apparently was quite profitable.

The trouble started when a man named John H. Smith went on a celebratory binge—either from a gold strike or his own engagement—that led to a drunken disagreement with Martha over a broken pitcher. He had entered the establishment and proceeded to knock the pitcher off the bar (whether he did so accidentally or on purpose was unclear).

Martha became angry and confronted Smith, at which the

pair became involved in a heated dispute. At some point, Smith apparently grabbed her and threw her roughly into a chair, whereupon Barclay came rushing in from the next room and drew his revolver, putting a bullet through Smith.

John Barclay was held briefly in the Columbia Jail before being forcibly removed by what amounted to a lynch mob. *Author photo*

The gunshot proved fatal.

The fact that Barclay had been defending his wife was no excuse in the eyes of the law, however. He was taken into custody and carted off to the hoosgow. But no sooner had he been deposited in the local lock-up than a mob of people began to gather, whipped up by a friend of the deceased named James W. Coffroth.

Coffroth was a prominent citizen: He served as president of the Columbia and Stanislaus River Water Company, which had been formed in 1854. He would later become a lawyer and serve in the State Senate.

But he was also, perhaps, not the fine and upstanding citizen he portrayed himself to be.

He lived a scant 100 feet from the saloon and had himself been a frequent customer—not only of Martha's drinking establishment, but of a boarding house she ran a block to the east, catty-corner to the jail at Jackson and Columbia streets. Martha would later recall showing him her own particular brand of "hospitality" in the person of a girl named Sally for whom he held a particular fondness.

But none of that prevented him from immediately accusing Barclay of murder and demanding that he answer for the crime with his life, as Martha later noted in a missive printed November 17, 1855, in the *Columbia Gazette*.

"Coffroth's memory will trace him back to the time when I kept a house, and he was a frequent visitor; nay, I should say, a steady boarder," she wrote. "But facts are stubborn things, and Coffroth would much rather not have me revert to the fact that he was the fancy man of one Sally who lived at my house."

Martha reported that she had often "kept my house open until one and two o'clock at night, for his especial benefit," allowing him to enter and leave by the back doors and windows at times.

"Often even at that late hour of night, oyster suppers were served for the Hon. Gentleman and his lady—and let me ask him who paid the bills, and whether one cent ever came out of his pocket? No! He was the recipient of many favors from a poor and wretched girl whose mother has often written her, imploring her to return home. Those letters Coffroth has read; and while others subscribed different sums in order to enable her to return to the arms of a broken hearted mother, Coffroth was not even the man to advise her to go home. He well knew that he would be too much the loser.

"He also forgets that whenever Sally left my house, on his account, he would come to me with tears in his eyes, and beg me to get her back again; and how often, when he would go out to ride with ladies of respectability, who knew not how contaminating he was, he would call me aside, and beg me to keep Sally from calling and speaking to him, while in the company of those ladies."

Martha even insinuated that Coffroth contracted syphilis or some other venereal disease as the result of his dalliances.

"He also forgets, that while laboring under the influence of a most loathsome disease, he went to San Francisco, leaving his lady here to starve, or die upon my hands. But Coffroth has a hold upon the worm, and now let him feel its bite."

Could this have been the true reason he called so vehemently for Barclay's death? Was it merely an excuse to exact revenge against the man's wife for his condition? Whatever his motives, Coffroth's self-righteous demands for "justice" in the form of Barclay's execution found resonance with the crowd.

By all accounts, the victim was widely liked.

Martha, by contrast, was not exactly an upstanding member of the community. (She merely protected the reputations of those who were, like Coffroth, and likely many others in the mob: There weren't many women on the frontier in those days, and there weren't many jobs for those without husbands who were there. And they had to make a living somehow.)

Whether for these reasons or merely because they were bloodthirsty, the mob needed no more encouragement than Coffroth's words. They rushed the jail where Barclay was being held, overpowering the town marshal and his officers. They brought a powder keg to the jail door and were prepared to blow it open, but managed to dislodge it through the use of axes, crowbars, and sledgehammers before any big blast was necessary.

It wasn't your typical vigilante justice: Wham, bam, hang the man! Instead, a semblance of a courtroom was assembled at the

Tuolumne County Water Company, with the *Columbia Clipper* newspaper editor being "sworn in" as judge on the spot. Still, it was a kangaroo court at best: Defense witnesses were not allowed to testify, while Coffroth was given free rein to hurl accusations at the defendant.

"There is a higher court to ask for mercy," he declared. "This man should fulfill the divine law of 'an eye for an eye, a tooth for a tooth, a life for a life.' 'Whosoever sheddeth a man's blood, by man shall his blood be shed.'"

This brought a round of applause from the clearly biased audience in attendance, accompanied by calls to "drag him up" and "hang him!" When it was argued that the entire proceeding was outside the law, cries arose of "Damn the laws!"

That's when the sheriff arrived, attempting to restore order... only to be seized by the throat and held back while a noose was placed around Barclay's neck under the water flume. Someone tried to cut him down, but was rewarded for his efforts by a blow to the head from the butt of a pistol.

Someone held a knife to the sheriff, and the execution proceeded, with Barclay strung up in a scene described in gruesome detail by the *Columbia Gazette*:

"The unfortunate Barclay was haltered, by a rope lowered from the flume, and those above hauled away upon it... No precautions were taken to pinion the victim, and he seized hold of the rope above his head, and held on to it with a grasp of desperation.

"Those above, raised him up suddenly and jerked him down, several times, but still the grasp of desperation held good. One of the executioners looked over the edge of the flume, and cried out, 'Let go, you damned fool, let go!' Finally, his strength gave out; one hand fell and then the other; drawing up his legs, he gave a few convulsive movements, and then hung straight; all was over; body and soul had parted. and his life being taken in recompense for the now doubly fatal act of defending his wife.

"Even at the time, the incident aroused a sense of shock and horror in the eyes of more sober-minded individuals."

In an editorial addressing the hanging, the *Gazette* posed the question: "We ask any man who looked on calmly (if any could do so) what chance any one stood for justice with the throng Wednesday? No reply is needed for us. The particulars that we give speak for themselves....

"It pains us to record these occurrences as having taken place in Columbia, and we would gladly omit them; but our duty as journalists compels us to publish them; they are a blot upon our town."

Barclay's body was returned to Chinese Camp, and one of the largest memorial services in the county's early history was held at St. Xavier's Catholic Church. Chinese Camp residents were so incensed that they lobbied for Columbia to be ousted from Tuolumne County.

As for his widow, Martha leased out her saloon to one Sam Mitchel immediately after her husband's death and sold it to him a year later. It was later renamed the Lone Star Saloon.

Martha remained a woman of some means, owning a brick house at Main and Pacific in Columbia by 1862. She married one James H. Hart in 1863 and moved to New Orleans sometime in the 1870s. She died at about the age of 43 in 1876; the cause of death was labeled as "general debility."

STEPHEN H. PROVOST

The Garrett House, founded around 1853, would be Chinese Camp's most prominent inn during the second half of the 19th century. *Tuolumne County Historical Society*

Boomtown Days

Many fortune-seekers traveling west sojourned for a time in Chinese Camp before moving on. The promise of richer diggings lured them down stream or down the road, or they stayed just long enough to realize the place wasn't for them. In fact, only six men listed in the 1850 town census were still around in 1853.

Occasionally, someone would arrive in Chinese Camp and disappear (intentionally or otherwise) altogether. An ad run in

October of 1854 in the *Shasta Courier* under a banner that read "Information Wanted," for instance, sought to determine the whereabouts of one William Kennedy. According to the ad, he was a Canadian man from Nova Scotia who, "when last heard from, was in the Chinese Diggings, southern mines. Any information of him will be thankfully received by L. Delap, Shasta city."

Was the ad placed by a concerned relative? Someone to whom he owed a debt? A bounty hunter determined to track him down? There's no way to know. The answer to those questions, as well as the ultimate whereabouts of Mr. Kennedy, remain a mystery. The ad ran for four successive weeks in October and early November, then... silence.

While some men were just passing through or disappearing, however, others saw fit to put down roots in Chinese Camp. By and large, these weren't miners—though they may have started out as such. Shrewd men knew that success in digging up gold could be fleeting, and some wanted something more permanent than tentpoles that had to be pulled up every few months in an endless search for better claims.

This is how camps became towns: A few men decided to trade their picks and sluice boxes for lives as merchants, saloon owners, blacksmiths, stage operators, and hoteliers. And most who did found this new, more sedentary life offered the benefit of a more stable income... as long as your business was fortunate enough to avoid the fires that swept through frontier towns all too frequently. Put simply, unless one hit a big bonanza, there was more money to be made catering to miners than actually mining.

From Kentucky to Crimea

One such gentleman was a lawyer from Jefferson County, Kentucky named James Wallace Kerrick. Kerrick left his law practice behind in 1851 to seek his fortune in California, accompanied by his eldest son and future son-in-law. He wound up near Chinese Camp, where he apparently had some success prospecting.

Encouraged, he returned home and collected his entire family: his wife Rachel, two daughters, and four sons, along with their wives and his oldest son's two children. Forming a train of nine ox-drawn wagons, they embarked on a nine-month trek in 1853 that led them across the Sonora Pass with horses, mules, 40 birds, and 150 cattle in tow.

Upon their safe arrival in Tuolumne County, Kerrick established a ranch near Green Springs, where he built a two-story structure with a wraparound porch. Christening it the "Kentucky House" in honor of his home state, he designed it to include accommodations for travelers complete with a livery stable, restaurant, and saloon. Weddings were even held there, and a stone corral, 2 feet thick and 5 feet high, was built on the site by Chinese laborers.

The Kentucky House, later known as the Crimea House, no longer stands, but its stone corral survives. *Author photo*

The Kentucky House served as a convenient stop for road-weary travelers at the junction of what's now called Red Hill Road and La Grange Road. Red Hill Road—then known as Mound Springs Road—runs about four miles north into Chinese Camp, where it was called Webster Avenue.

Travelers could also reach Chinese Camp from the south via the Sonora Road, roughly the same as State Route 120. At the community of Keystone, the road turned north after traveling east from the northern San Joaquin Valley. From there, it continued north to Jamestown and Sonora.

A third important road was the Milton-China Creek Road, which took wagons east from Milton to Copperopolis, then southeast from there into Chinese Camp. From there, you could travel north to Sonora, south to Coulterville, or east to Big Oak Flat and Yosemite.

Yosemite Junction, about four miles west of Chinese Camp, was where the wagon roads that became State Routes 108 and 120 converged in a three-road split. J.W. Goodwin founded a travelers' stop there in 1854, and you see some more recent abandoned buildings there today.

With all these roads heading into Chinese Camp, the town itself was like the hub of a wheel: You could get virtually anywhere you wanted to go from there.

That made it a convenient, bustling waystation... but it had its drawbacks, as well. As a key crossroads way station it was naturally prone to attract trouble, and a particular sort of trouble started nearby along San Antonio Creek around midnight on November 1, 1856.

According to an account in the *San Andreas Independent*, "two Mexicans entered the tents of some Chinamen and after intimidation, by threats, succeeded in robbing them of $40, in coin; all they had. An American, in a cabin close by, saw them mount their horses and ride off. He attempted to defend the

Chinamen, and having only an axe, made poor progress. The alarm was also extended to the store, but too late, as the thieves were already over the hill and out of sight."

This disturbance took place less than two months after two rival Chinese groups, or tongs, had gathered at the site for a major armed confrontation (which will be discussed in more detail later). Whether or not these events had any influence on Kerrick, he was approaching 60 and likely already feeling the effects of tuberculosis.

Regardless of his motive, Kerrick sold the business that same year and retired to a ranch near Collegeville, where his son had built a similar waystation on the Sonora Road called Kerrick's or 8-Mile House. He passed away in October of the following year, but the Kentucky House continued to operate for many years, the new owner changing the name to "Crimea House" (possibly a reference to the Crimean War being fought at the time). It was lost to fire in 1949, but the stone corral that dates from its early years can still be seen near the crossroads.

Sims Ranch

Another early pioneer who settled near, but not quite in Chinese Camp was John Sims.

Sims arrived in 1848 Sims and married Bridget Sims, a widow from Ireland with an infant daughter, around 1853. (She was just 20 or 21 years old at the time and would die young at about 40 years of age in 1873.) Sims' brothers Robert and James also settled in Chinese Camp, while another brother, Henry, would open a saloon and bunkhouse at Chinese Station along the Sierra Railway line.

The Sims family founded Sims Ranch, sometimes known as Dutch Ranch, a little west of town, where Sims Road offers a beautiful springtime drive through rolling hills along a picturesque creek for much of its length. Its endpoints are

Wildflowers bloom along Sims Road. *Author photo*

Highway 49 in the north and Red Hill Road in the south—crossing Highway 120 about halfway between the two.

One of the most bizarre incidents reported from the early days of Chinese Camp took place at Dutch Ranch sometime in the 1850s.

Recounted by a pioneer some years later, the episode involved a stolen knife, a grisly murder at the ranch, and a startling discovery that the owner of the knife (the pioneer) kept secret for a very long time... perhaps until he recounted it to a group of fellow old-timers sitting around a stove one day.

The story appeared in the *Stockton Evening Mail* in 1888.

"Talking of Bowie knives," he said, "I brought a beauty with me from Philadelphia when I came here, as one of a trading company, in the spring of '50. It had a lignum vitae handle, ornamented with silver, and I was mighty proud of it."

His company pitched their tents on Stockton's Center Street, and the pioneer took a run up to Sonora. He hadn't been there long, however, when he received word that "everything was not going right in our camp" and returned.

Arriving at nightfall, he set himself up for the night in a covered wagon ("which was a better bed than I could get in the city"). He took the knife out of his boot and put it in a leather pouch that was swung from the inside of the wagon, which he used to hold tools like hammers and wrenches.

After spending the next two days taking in the city and settling business matters, he returned with the intent of heading back to Sonora.

That's when he discovered the knife was missing.

"I knew there was no use in hunting for it," he said, "so I gave up and left."

The missing knife was largely forgotten and might have faded from the pioneer's memory altogether had he not gotten wind of a shocking episode at the Sims place sometime later.

"About a year or more afterwards," he recalled, "a man was murdered—cut to pieces, in fact—in his tent at Dutch Ranch, about two miles below Chinese Camp. I was living in Jimtown at the time, and happened to pay a visit to a friend of mine, who kept a saloon and express office in Chinese Camp. The murder was all the talk, and the knife which the murderer used was shown to me, covered in blood.

"It was my own knife! I recognized it at once by two cracks across the handle, caused by the shrinking of the wood in the California heat, and by two peculiar notches in the sheath, which kept it from falling out when carried in the belt.

"Did I claim it? Not much! And yet I don't know why. No one would have suspected me of being the murderer, for I could have easily proven my alibi by scores of witnesses. But yet I never admired my knife less than I did at that moment, and what became of it I never knew, nor did I particularly care.

"But I should have like to have seen that murderer caught and lynched, for the chances are that he was the thief that stole my knife from the wagon."

Building on the Boom

In Chinese Camp itself, the community was transforming itself quickly from a tent encampment into a town with permanent structures.

The first store in town was described sometime later as a large log cabin that housed both the mercantile and the owner's living quarters. Built on Main Street, it stood just to one side of the red-brick express company office. In 1924, the *Oakland Tribune* described the memory of it as follows:

"Logs were none too plentiful on that flat, so [the owner] built the walls up but five feet, then rigged up a framework of poles and fastened over it some old tent cloth and sacks. In the way of fixtures, he had a large log split in half for a counter. The other half was used as a bench for customers to sit on. No shelves were necessary, for all the goods were sold from the original package... He had no flooring, except that provided by mother nature."

Although he made his living selling goods to miners, the storekeeper knew a good opportunity when he saw one. And if he was scrupulous about keeping his store clean, his motive went beyond an affinity for tidiness, for he was less than scrupulous in dealing with some of his customers.

This was gold country, after all.

"He was a very cleanly storekeeper; every night after closing up he carefully swept up the floor in front of and behind the counter, and every night he carefully panned this dust for the other dust he knew would be in it, for he was a very careless man when he was handling other fellows' gold dust.

"He had a habit of accidentally striking his right elbow at just the right moment to spill a few grams over the counter or wipe up a little now and then by brushing his shirt sleeve carelessly across an exposed pile of fine gold. It was wonderful how careless he was at times."

As the town grew, the storekeeper was put out of business by larger and better-stocked merchants. Among them were Mason & Company and Vedder & Company, both of which set up shop in more permanent masonry buildings.

Other businessmen followed.

The Eagle and the Garrett House hotels were founded around 1853, and by the following year, one Richard Marshall was using the Garrett House as headquarters where one might inquire of "valuable mining claims" for sale on the Tuolumne River.

The Eagle was run by a man named Waltze, and the more well-known Garrett House was founded by brothers Hiram and "Stovepipe Pete" Garrett. The two-story building would eventually come under the proprietorship of a man named Solinsky.

Like J.W. Kerrick, Solinsky came to the area as a miner. An early arrival, his name was among six on the 1850 census list who stuck around more than a couple years. His full name was impressively long—Christian William Hugo Solinsky—and he carried an equally impressive title to go with it. The Count, as he was known, really was one. Born in 1814, he'd come to the United States from Poland, fearing he would be exiled to Siberia for fighting in the November Uprising of 1830 against Russia.

Following his arrival, Solinsky enlisted in the U.S. Navy and then in the Army, fighting in the 1846 war with Mexico. Initially returning to Pennsylvania at the war's conclusion, he embarked two years later on a sea voyage around Cape Horn on the ship Oceola, which brought him to California in the summer of 1849.

"California and its gold are all the go," the *Miners' Journal* enthused in January of 1849. "Thousands are rushing to the newly discovered El Dorado, where they hope to accumulate enough gold to secure them a handsome fortune. Among others who have gone to California, we observe the following names from Schuylkill county—They sailed on Tuesday morning last on the

Oceola: Brevet Capt. C.W.H. Solinsky..."

On arriving, the count tried his hand at prospecting in Calaveras and Mariposa counties before finding his way to Chinese Camp.

Whether his endeavors as a miner yielded much success is not known, but it is clear that by 1850, he had opted to change directions and try a different occupation, signing on as an agent for the Adams & Company Express line alongside a partner named Sol Miller.

Count Solinsky in a portrait from his younger years. *Tuolumne County Historical Society*

Miller, a native of Berks County in Pennsylvania, arrived in California in 1849 at about the age of 20. After initially working the mines in Jacksonville, he struck it rich at Angels Camp before heading to San Francisco and starting a business there with partner P.K. Aurand. But a fire destroyed their business in May of 1850, so the pair returned to Tuolumne County and opened a mercantile called Montezuma House, around which grew the eponymous mining camp of Montezuma.

Less than two months after relocating, however, Miller was hit with another misfortune: On June 29, 1850, three Mexican customers entered his store and purchased goods. They paid for them... but then proceeded to pull out a long knife and stab him three times. One of the wounds went all the way through his body, puncturing both lungs, another was in the neck, and a third in the arm.

The robbers also wounded his partner, who awoke near him with a single question on his lips: "Sol, I am stabbed," he said. "Are you alive?"

Miller survived, but Aurand did not.

The two were found the next morning, and Miller was taken to the home of a judge for convalescence. A silver lining to the whole affair was the fact that the bandits had made off with only $300, having failed to discover $7,000 Miller and Aurand had hidden in a bread barrel.

That left Miller enough money to embark on a new endeavor, and it was shortly after that when he formed his partnership with Solinsky at Chinese Camp.

At a Crossroads

Mining aside, it was Chinese Camp's location as a major stopping point on the road from one place to another that was the key to its prominence. Road-building was important, as it allowed miners to get their gold from one place to another and merchants to bring in goods to sell to those self-same miners.

A man named John Caruthers had built a toll road between Sonora and Stockton in 1854, becoming the main route between the port city and the Southern Mines. But even before that, stage operators were offering service between the two areas.

In 1850, a line called Todd & Company was boasting it offered the only service to the Southern Mines, teaming up with Adams & Company with the intent of offering daily stages to destinations including Jamestown, Mokelumne Hill, San Andreas, and Sonora.

Adams Express eventually absorbed the Todd line, and it was with this company that Solinsky and Miller took employment. But it was hardly the only game in town. As mentioned earlier, Reynolds Express had been running passenger service to "all parts of the Southern Mines south of the Stanislaus River" since

Stagecoaches

Some coaches held five passengers, some eight, some eleven, some fourteen. Some coaches were driven by four horses, some by five, three abreast at the lead, and some by six horses, with a swing pole for the two center horses.

A well-organized stage line which operated a number of coaches had the same inspection of its coaches as has a railroad car, or a motor vehicle stage... The old stage road was full of loose rocks, bumps, tree roots, ditches, water breaks and all kinds of obstacles to shake one up at times.

The horses on a stage line were selected from among the hardy breeds, and those which could stand the daily grind in order to fill the time schedule, averaging ten to fifteen miles per hour. A change of horses was necessary every ten to fifteen miles; for instance, from Chinese Camp to Yosemite Valley, a distance of 60 miles, there were five change stations to take care of each coach.

Paul Morris, 1943

The life of a stage driver was a happy go lucky one. The occupation lasted from May to October. For six months the salary was from $50 to $75 per month with room and board. In the winter, they would accept employment breaking young horses for the coming summer at a salary of about one-half what they got in the summer.

Paul Morris, 1926

September of 1950. But there was no guarantee that this service—which ran daily from Sonora through Chinese Camp to Coulterville—would be entirely by stage: In bad weather, when the road washed out, passengers would have to mount up on horse or mule the rest of the way. (The animal was provided at no additional charge, but a second animal to haul baggage cost you extra.)

Reynolds remained in operation until 1853, when it was purchased by Wells Fargo—setting up a fierce rivalry with the Adams company that would continue for the next couple of years. By that time, a stage was running on the road between Sonora and Chinese Camp every two or three hours.

The Big Oak Flat Road was already being built in 1850, but at that point only ran from a few miles west of Chinese Camp to a few miles east of it, at Shepley's Flat. By 1856, the road had been extended and widened enough for heavy freight, making the steep ascent up Priest's Grade to Big Oak Flat and Groveland. Four years later, it had reached Second Garotte, a few miles farther east, on its way to Yosemite.

"In the good old days of staging, the Old Priest's Hill—which was later abandoned and a new grade established—was the one traversed," Chinese Camp merchant and stage line owner Paul Morris recalled. "It was a long, dreary, hard pull on the stage horses and very tiresome on the weary stage passengers. It often gave the passengers the inspiration to feel sorry for the poor stage horses, and many got out and walked up Priest's Hill. A good appetite was always with one when the top was reached."

W.C. Priest—the first park commissioner at Yosemite—and his wife Margaret owned the hotel at the summit, and he had been instrumental in constructing the Big Oak Flat Toll Road as superintendent of the Great Sierra Stage Company.

Margaret and her first husband, Alexander Kirkwood, had established a mining supply store at the summit in 1853. After he died young, leaving her a widow, she received three dozen proposals of marriage from would-be suitors. She accepted W.C. Priest's offer.

Margaret Priest had a reputation as a warm and attentive

host... but she had some help getting ready for guests in the form of a pet shepherd dog, which a traveler from Scotland offered to train for her.

She took him up on the offer.

It wasn't just a matter of teaching the pup to fetch the newspaper or something so simple. Instead, he trained the shepherd to leave the hotel every evening and head down to the base of the hill around sundown, when the stages were set to arrive. Each driver would write on a scrap of paper the number of passengers on board his stage and affix it to the dog's couple, sending the messenger back up the hill with the information.

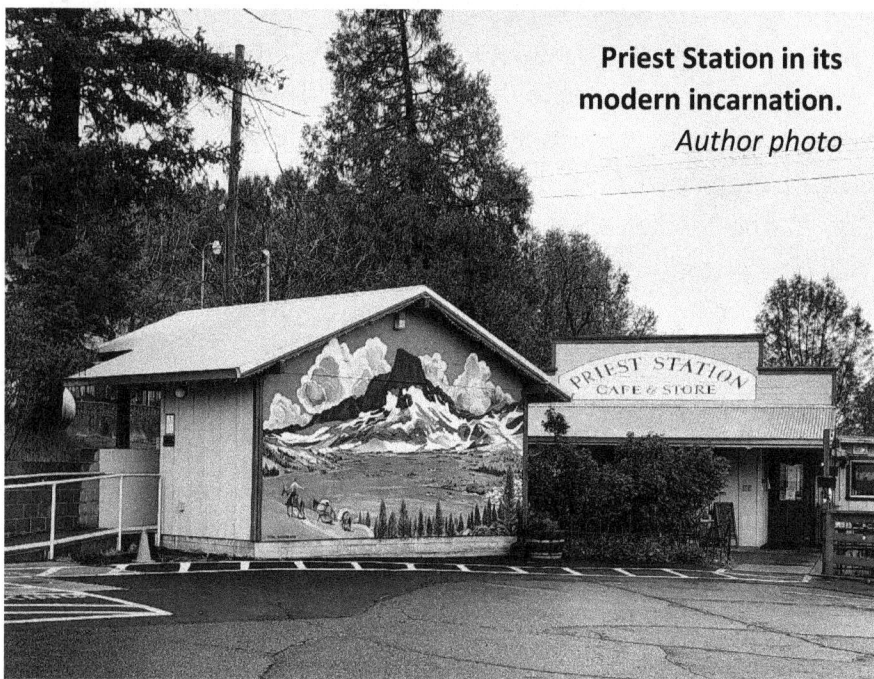

Priest Station in its modern incarnation.
Author photo

The stages needed to rest their horses frequently on the steep grade and water them at troughs halfway up the hill, so the shepherd had no trouble beating them back to the hotel—usually by more than an hour.

That gave Mrs. Priest plenty of time to prepare a room and a table for her guests before they arrived. (Sadly, the 22-building

Priest Hotel burned to the ground in 1926, leaving a well as the only remaining structure. The hotel was rebuilt, passed into other hands, but was repurchased by the Anker family, descendants of the Priests, in 2007.)

Despite its harrowing climb to Priest Hotel at the summit, the road became popular not only for hauling freight but among adventurers seeking to experience the beauty of the Sierra in and around Yosemite Valley. Such demand made Chinese Camp even more popular as a waystation for travelers between Stockton and Groveland.

Once you got to First Garotte, as it was called back then, you could stop for provisions at the Granite Store, founded in 1852 and now known as the Iron Door Saloon. The 16½-mile journey up from Chinese Camp might not seem like much today, but given the condition of the road and the steepness of the climb, it was a good idea to get a good night's sleep under one's belt before attempting it back in the 1850s.

This being the case, it's not surprising that rooms in Chinese Camp were booked solid a couple of days out. That's not to mention the stages coming down from Sonora, wagons heading up from the southwest on Mound Springs Road (Red Hill Road), and travelers taking the shortcut to Sonora via Poverty Hill.

All this put men like Solinsky and Miller in the catbird's seat to make a fine living at the center of a bustling crossroads town. When Adams & Company failed in the area, they simply switched their affiliation to Pacific Express and then to Wells Fargo, controlling freight and passenger traffic through the heart of the Southern Mines and serving as branch agents of San Francisco's Frenz & Ralston banking concern as well, handling shipments of gold dust and nuggets.

The pair remained in business together until 1870 and, at one point, had expanded their concern to include offices in Big Oak Flat, Chinese Camp, Coulterville, Don Pedro Bar, and Montezuma.

Miller spent two terms as tax collector and also served as undersheriff before leaving for Stockton in 1871 and San Francisco in 1875. There he served as solicitor for Spruance, Stanley & Co. and, according to one account, "achieved a wide celebrity in his business."

Miller at one point lived in what Dr. Stratton's wife described as "probably the most pretentious house in town." It stood on a knoll at the east end of Washington Street, next to what's now Highway 49 and across from the Odd Fellows Hall—near the current site of the small Odd Fellows Cemetery. Unfortunately, like so many other historic buildings in town, it was lost to fire.

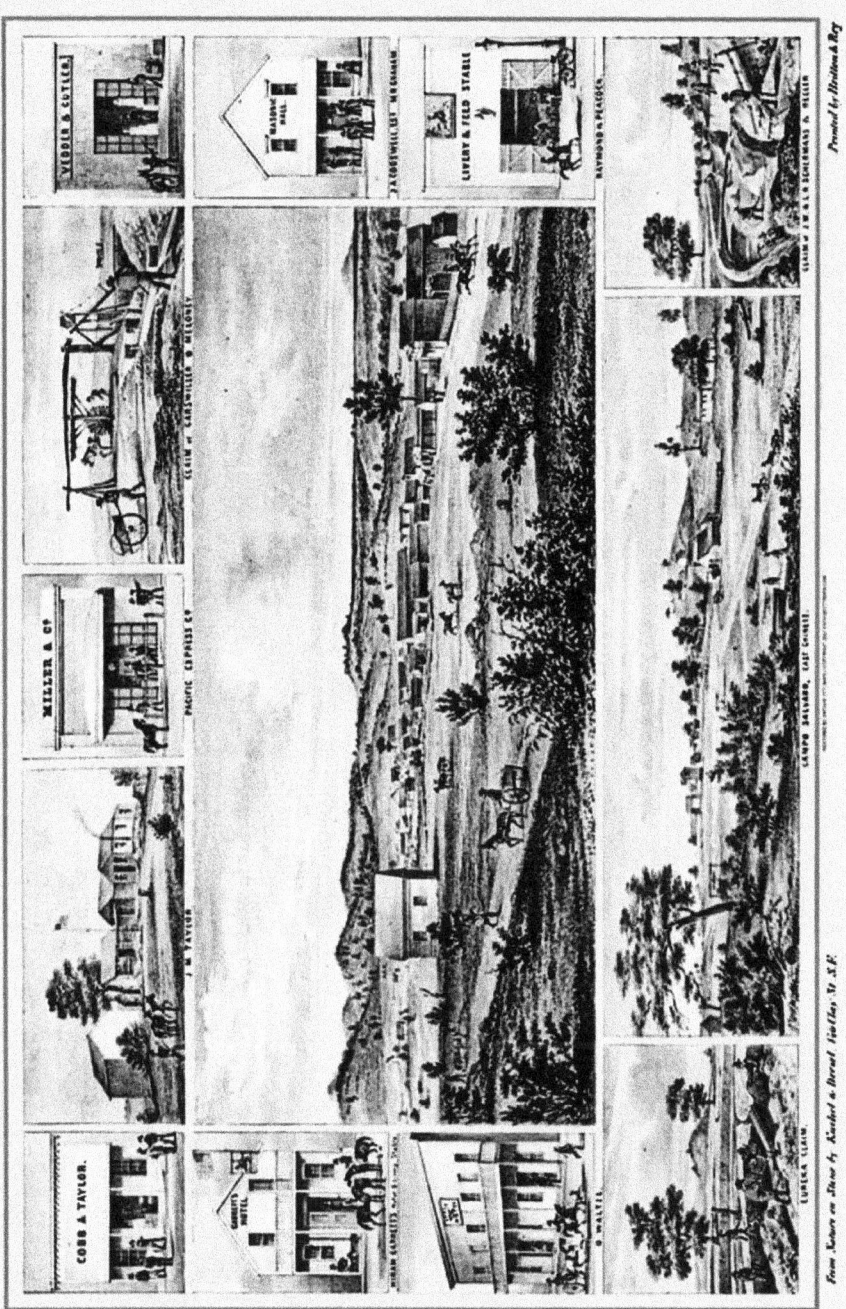

Chinese Camp in 1856. None of the buildings showcased in the perimeter sketches (which include a panorama of Campo Salvado) still stand.

St. Xavier's Catholic Church, on a hill overlooking Chinese Camp, was in place by 1855. *Author photo*

1856

The year 1856 saw Chinese Camp reach perhaps its peak of influence and commerce. There were, not surprisingly, two saloons operating, along with three butcher shops, two jewelers (for those who wanted their gold set right away), a grocer, two druggists, and three doctors.

It was, in short, no longer a "camp," but a "town."

The total population in '56, recorded in the *Heckendorn & Wilson Directory*, was listed at 1,000 persons. But that wasn't counting the Chinese population, which was likely several times that large.

The town had, by this time, divided itself into clear ethnic sections along a small cross-thatched network of roadways running roughly north to south and east to west—mostly to the west of modern Highway 49. The main north-south artery was (and is) Red Hill Road, which was called Webster Avenue in the 1800s, and which largely marked the dividing line between the white and Chinese sections of town.

Other north-south roads through the western, Chinese, section were Broadway and Church Street. Main and Washington streets ran parallel to each other east and west through both sections, with a third (now defunct) street called Empire farthest north.

Up the hill, east of the modern highway, St. Xavier's Catholic Church and cemetery overlooked the city across Main Street from a little one-room schoolhouse. The original church building was in the center of town, but residents wanted a bigger sanctuary, so they built a new one to the east. The floor of the original church was carried up the hill to become part of the new one, and a priest named Father Aleric conducted the first Mass there, serving a congregation of 70 members, in 1855.

The church, now boarded up, still stands, but the old schoolhouse that stood nearby is gone: The original building was moved into town to serve as a saloon, of all things, and its replacement burned in 2006. (A modern school built in the 1970s with Chinese-themed architecture sits just south of town on Red Hill Road.)

Stage owner and shopkeeper Paul Morris recalled it was "a common sight" to see "10 or more 12-horse freight teams in the Camp overnight, the town being [the] divergent point for Sonora and Big Oak Flat sections."

At the start of 1856, the town's freight and tourist traffic had created such demand that two new hotels had opened. In addition to the Eagle and Garrett House, H. Mattison had opened the Belvidere, and Ramon and Peacock were operating the El

Dorado. Neither would last nearly as long as the Garrett.

"Algerine, Montezuma, and Chinese Camp were the largest and most important of the mining camps in the early days," Lee Whipple-Haslam would recall. "Mining progressed very rapidly. Montezuma and Chinese Camp became emporiums of trade. All kinds of businesses flourished."

In addition to the hospitality industry, blacksmithing was a natural money-maker. Five blacksmiths and two livery stables were operating in town that year, shoeing horses and providing shelter for saddle and carriage animals—serving much the same function that automotive garages would in the early years of car travel.

A sign advertises Louis Egling's business as blacksmith and undertaker with the distance (4 miles) to Chinese Camp, c. 1905.

Foremost among them was Louis Egling, who'd arrived from Germany at the age of 22 and set up a wheelwright shop in 1852. He didn't just shoe horses. He built wagons, stages, and freight-haulers, too. Such was his skill and reputation that he attracted a number of employees to serve as assistants: enough to keep six forges running as they forged mining implements such as picks and shovels along with farming tools and nails, among other things.

Egling even built coffins and served as the town undertaker.

Among the other diverse things that came out of Egling's shop were wheelbarrows. This is significant in light of his grandson's recollection that one of Egling's helpers was none other than John Studebaker, whose name would ultimately adorn the famous automobile. Though impossible to confirm, it's not outside the realm of possibility: Studebaker did, in fact, work making wheelbarrows up in Placerville before moving back east and founding the company that would eventually produce... well... Studebakers.

Egling's clients included Galen Clark, the conservationist who came to California in 1854 and successfully advocated for legislation to protect Yosemite Valley. He moved to Wawona and became known as the park's guardian.

Egling crafted one of his Egling wagons for Clark, and his shop also built the iron truss rods for a new bridge at Knight's Ferry after a flood destroyed the first bridge there in 1862.

Thomas Vinson, a stonemason also from Chinese Camp, built the piers for that same bridge.

Egling expanded his operations to include a satellite blacksmith shop in Columbia and would eventually move to Angels Camp before passing away in 1934.

The stone remains of Louis Egling's granary, as seen from Maiden Lane. *Author photo*

Louis Egling's blacksmith and wagon shop is quiet today (author photo, top), but it was abuzz with activity in an 18th century photo courtesy of Richard Beale (above).

Above: Main Street looking east in 1930 from Red Hill Road. Louis Egling once owned property just this side of the Morris duplex seen at right. *University of California Libraries and California Historical Society*

Below: An entry by Egling in Saul Morris' autograph book dated 1883. *Richard Beale collection*

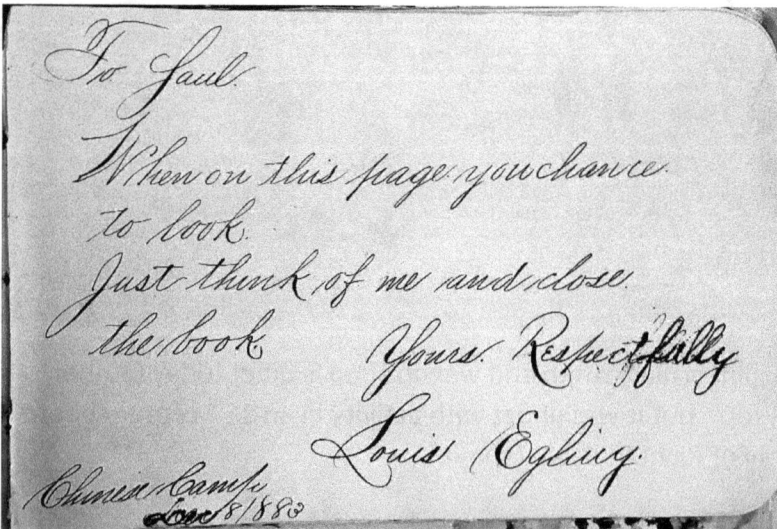

DR. R. M. LAMPSON,
PHYSICIAN AND SURGEON,
CHINESE CAMP.

HAVING PURCHASED THE DRUG
Store formerly kept by Dr. J. A. Bogle, I wish to
inform the Public that I have removed from Monteznma
and heraafter will have my office at Chinese Camp.
All kinds of Drugs and Medicines constantly on hand.

☞ PRESCRIPTIONS carefully Compounded. ☜

R. M. LAMPSON, M. D.

Chinese Camp. June 4, 1870—tf

Medicine... Such as it Was

A series of physicians worked in Chinese Camp, including a man named James C. Peacock, who earned his medical degree in Philadelphia before heading west in 1850.

He was about 40 years old when he got to Chinese Camp, where he became "a prosperous and wealthy merchant," partnering with a friend named Captain Raymond in ventures that included the El Dorado Hotel (where the devastating fire of 1856 broke out) and a livery stable.

His success enabled him to purchase a ranch at Dickerson's Ferry on the Tuolumne River in Stanislaus County. But even amid his many business endeavors, he continued to practice medicine: the state register and year book listed him as the physician for Chinese Camp as late as 1859.

By the following year, Peacock had departed. He and Raymond bought some land near Mariposa, where they established a ranch on Chowchilla Creek.

In their absence, J.A. Bogle set up a practice and pharmacy on the north side of Main Street, just east of the New York Store. Bogle was likely the physician called upon to treat the wife of Joseph Whyte, a prominent citizen who had come from Ireland with his brothers John and Thomas to mine for gold and settled in

Chinese Camp around 1850.

The Whyte brothers must have done very well by themselves, because they were able to buy a sprawling ranch that straddled the Tuolumne-Calaveras county line and extended all the way from near Green Springs to northeast of Oakdale.

During this time, they wrote a series of letters to family members back in Ireland, one of which told of Mrs. Joseph Whyte's heartbreaking death despite the doctor's valiant attempts to save her.

Mrs. Whyte passed away not from any of the ailments that were all too common in the day, such as consumption or dropsy, but rather during childbirth. Joseph recalled the events that surrounding her passing in a correspondence addressed to his two sisters, Mary and Teresa:

"We considered it would be better for her to remove from the ranch to Chinese Camp for these reasons:

"First, the doctor, who attended her before and who is a very eminent physician, said that unless he could be with her immediately after the first symptoms of labour set in, that he would not bring a living child. The doctor resides in Chinese; it is 10 miles from our place and his coming would cause a delay of 4 or 5 hours.

"Second, her cousin—the only relative she had in the state—lives in Chinese and pressed her so much to go and got up a beautiful room for her accommodation.

"Third, the church is also in Chinese, so that she would only have to walk a few steps to Mass. It was hard on both of us to separate at that particular time, but I had to go to market in Chinese twice a week, so I saw her almost every other day...

"On the Saturday [before] her death, I was in Chinese, and she said she was sure her sickness was coming on and wished me to stay with her, so I remained. She felt well on Sunday; [then,] about 12 o'clock on Monday, her labor came on."

The doctor and nurse arrived immediately, but the patient

was afflicted with sharp pains. Distraught and in severe pain, she pleaded twice with her husband to kiss her, then uttered a soft prayer. Then, suddenly, she convulsed in a spasm, and not three minutes later, died in her husband's arms, "like a baby going to sleep."

The child, however, never came.

Some people tried to console the grieving widower by saying it was best that the baby had not been born into the world without its mother.

But Joseph dismissed this as "false reasoning." The fact

Gravestone of Thomas Whyte at St. Xavier's Catholic Church. Thomas, who shares a plot with Hanora M. Whyte, lived until 1890. *Author photo*

was, he said, his wife was gone with "nothing left to represent" her, making "the sad event still sadder."

He closed his "melancholy epistle" by expressing deep thanks to this "American friends of Chinese Camp" for the kindness and sympathy extended to him. "Those men came to me in my affliction and, when they found they could not console me, they entered into my grief and cried like children."

He then assured his sisters that "the sharp pangs of grief are fast wearing off, and I begin to have some relish for life."

Joseph Whyte would live 43 more years, passing away in 1907

at the age of 77. He and his brothers are buried in the St. Xavier's Cemetery, adjacent to the church in Chinese Camp.

J.A. Bogle, meanwhile, maintained his practice and drugstore in Chinese Camp until 1870, when it was purchased by one R.M. Lampson, who came to town after several years serving Montezuma. Lampson would remain in town until Daniel Stratton bought his home and practice around 1889.

A native of Vermont, Lampson was about 20 years old when he arrived in Montezuma, around 1852, working as a miner for the next five years before turning to medicine. He would eventually serve two terms in the State Senate and also supported his friend Prentice Mulford's copper mining enterprise sometime in the early 1860s as a member of his company, which was formed at Bob Love's store in Montezuma.

Mulford recalled the company and his association with Lampson in *A History of Tuolumne County*, published in 1882:

"I wrote the constitution and by-laws. I fitted the company out on paper with a president, a secretary, a treasurer and a board of directors, and also with a 'prospector.' I was the prospector.

"The prospector was really the company. The prospector did all the work, discovered all the claims, kept them up, collected all the monthly assessments I could from some thirty members, living over an area of territory larger than the State of Connecticut, and officiated per proxy as president, treasurer, secretary and board of directors...

"The active working force of the company consisted of a very poor horse, a very poor dog and very inferior shot-gun, whose energies were largely expended at the breech in kicking me when I fired, a frying-pan, a coffee-pot, a small stock of provisions and a pair of blankets."

Those who supported him did so in the form of a loan for the horse and saddle, which he obtained in exchange for company stock. Then there were those 30 company members from whom he collected assessments. Whether Lampson was an investor or an assessed member (or both), Mulford wrote glowingly of the doctor's contributions and character.

He wrote: "Among the more prominent members of my company, whose memories with me now rank among my greatest earthly treasures, were Dr. Lampson, of Chinese Camp, a whole-souled man, full of generosity, good will, and, in his profession, good acts for his fellow man, as many a miner can testify."

As good a doctor as Lampson apparently was, however, medical care in those days wasn't exactly up to modern standards.

A dispatch from the *Nevada Democrat* reported that a man had broken his leg at Chinese Camp a few days earlier. The limb was set, but the man continued to complain of pain. The doctor therefore applied chloroform... "from the effects of which the man died in a few hours."

Doubtless he would have preferred enduring the pain from his broken leg.

Fire and War

A panorama of the town produced in 1856 by Kuchel and Dresel is surrounded by individual sketches showing the two-story Eagle Hotel—with six windows across behind a second-floor balcony—as well as the smaller Garrett House.

Other frames display the Raymond and Peacock Livery Stable, a two-story Masonic Lodge, Miller and Solinsky's Pacific Express Office, and two merchant locations: Vedder & Cutler and Cobb & Taylor. Still others show various mining operations, and at the bottom of the picture (shown at the end of the previous chapter) is a panorama of Camp Salvado.

Unfortunately, none of the buildings pictured in the lithograph have survived.

One reason is a series of fires, the first of which roared through town in the summer of this, perhaps Chinese Camp's most prosperous year. The conflagration broke out in the El Dorado Hotel and, according to the *Amador Ledger*, "destroyed the entire portion of Main street between Mr. Gamble's store and the store occupied by Brock & Blake."

The only buildings spared along that stretch were Miller and Solinsky's Pacific Express Office directly opposite the hotel, and the fireproof Vedder & Cutler building.

Losses included $6,500 to the Garrett House and $2,000 to the Eagle Hotel. In all, 33 properties were reported damaged, with the total cost coming in at $74,000—far more than $2 million in modern currency.

The good news is that the community was prosperous enough to rebuild. This would not be the case in the future, once Chinese Camp entered into a period of decline, but for now mining and stagecoach driving were at or near their peak, and there was every incentive to start over again with hardier and more durable materials.

"Chinese Camp has arisen from its ashes, and will soon be one of the most beautiful towns in the Southern mines." So began a letter signed by a certain John to the *Sonora Union Democrat* at the end of August 1856. "Fireproof buildings, mostly brick, take the place of the old dilapidated buildings that were burnt down, while every portion of the town shows a marked improvement: the result of the perseverance of its citizens."

The fire notwithstanding, the most noteworthy event of 1856 in the vicinity of Chinese Camp happened a few miles south of town, near where Mound Springs Road and La Grange Road intersected at Crimea House.

Two neighboring groups of Chinese were working on adjacent claims at Two-Mile Bar on the Stanislaus River when it happened. There was no love lost between the two groups, which hailed from different districts back in China long engaged in a

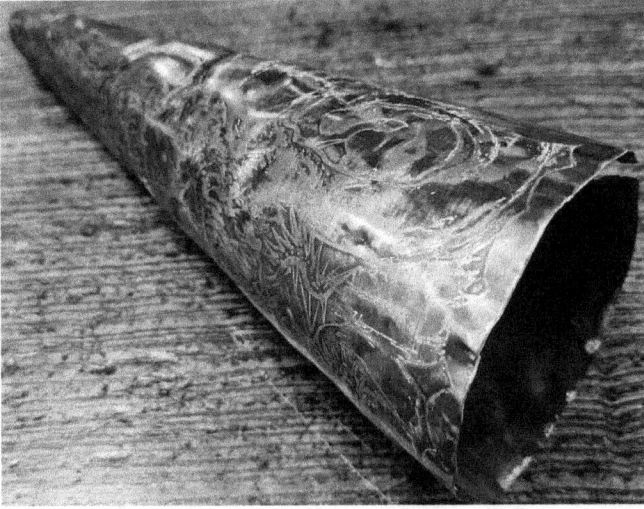

This metal horn, with the figure of a dragon etched into one side, was found at the site of the 1856 Tong War. *Richard Beale collection*

bitter rivalry or feud. So when a boulder from the Sam Yap group rolled onto the Yang Wo claim, all hell broke loose.

According to one account, Yang Wo miners took exception and demanded it be removed, but their neighbors adamantly refused. According to another, the boulder contained a sizable gold nugget, in which case it would seem that the beneficiary would have wanted to keep it.

Regardless, the boulder—whether a prize or a nuisance—remained where it was, and an argument broke out between the two groups. The Sam Yap group, with a dozen men at the site, lost no time in ousting the Yang Wo contingent (which was half its size) from their claim on the river's south bank. But that was far from the end of the matter.

The displaced Yang Wo prospectors promptly sent out word to others from their clan in Chinese Camp, Camp Salvado, and Peppermint and Slumgullion gulches... and the Sam Yap contingent called up reinforcements of their own.

Things were escalating, and quickly, toward a battle. The site of the encounter was set for a field near La Grange and Mound Springs roads. One of the groups built a large stone fort, and both at once commenced seeking ways to train and arm themselves.

This historical marker commemorates the Tong War at Red Hill Road just off La Grange Road, the site of the Crimea House, which burned down on Oct. 8, 1949. *Author photo*

The Sam Yap group enlisted the help of 15 white advisors, presumably with military experience, to serve as drill instructors. Their compensation? Ten dollars a day, plus all the food they could eat and as much whiskey as they could drink. (That $10 was not an insignificant sum, amounting to roughly $250 in today's dollars.)

Not only did these advisors prepare the group for battle, they also apparently took part in the combat itself as "ringers," painting themselves yellow, donning Chinese attire, and dangling horsehair down their back to approximate the pigtails worn in the day.

Neither side was equipped with—or well versed in using—modern firearms, so the Sam Yap group bought 150 muskets and bayonets, which they had shipped in from San Francisco. Both sides, meanwhile, put in urgent orders with blacksmiths across the region to forge any kind of weapon they could come up with. Louis Egling in Chinese Camp crafted a number of spears and knives used in the confrontation.

When the time finally came for the two sides to meet, it was quite a spectacle, drawing somewhere between 2,500 and 5,000 combatants (indicating just how many Chinese immigrants had settled in the area), while large numbers of white residents turned out as well, eager to witness the fray. It all took place on a Sunday, and there was every bit as much interest then as there would be in a professional football game today.

As the *Columbia Gazette* recounted shortly afterward, "The ground was well selected, affording a good view to the spectators... There were several hundred Americans present, who posted themselves on the surrounding heights, all, no doubt, expecting to see a 'pitch-fork' fight in perfect security."

(This sense of security would, however, be unceremoniously shattered when one of the groups began firing musket balls over their heads!)

The *Gazette*, which referred to the two sides as the "Canton party"—apparently the Sam Yap group—and the "Hong Kong party," offered a vivid account of what happened that day:

"We started for the battle ground at an early hour on the day appointed, and on arriving at Chinese Camp, we fell in with the Hong Kong party, numbering about three hundred and armed with almost every barbarous weapon imaginable, including guns, pistols, knives, lances (from eight to twenty feet in length), three-tined pitch-forks, javelins, and clubs.

"At about eight o'clock, the 'Legion' took up the line of march for the field, preceded by their Captains and banner bearers, mounted and on foot. Other companies joined them on the way, increasing their number to about four hundred.

The racist caricature was used by the post office to commemorate the 80th anniversary of the Tong War in 1936. (Note postmaster Helen Stratton's signature below the image.) The ink stamp itself is seen at right.
Richard Beale collection

"We kept on the road, in the direction from which the Canton party were expected, and a few miles below Mound Springs we met them 'in martial array,' with triangular banners of almost every color and design, 'waving o'er' them. At this time, they had received news of the enemy's approach, and prepared to receive them by throwing out small bodies of men to the right and left, to take 'the foe in flank.'"

Once the two sides caught sight of each other, they appeared at first hesitant to engage.

"The opposing armies marched up in fine style to within less than half a mile of each other, but did not appear over anxious to come to close quarters," the *Gazette* recounted. "A party of musketeers from the Canton party were posted in the woods to the south of the field and kept up irregular fire for some time without any effect, but finally the Hong Kongs got their dander up and started to dislodge them, when a stray ball struck their leader, and he fell.

"This discouraged them, and the Cantons, taking advantage of the moment, charged in regular Oriental style, and such screaming and yelling we have never before heard, and never expect to hear again, unless there is another Chinese fight in the neighborhood.

"They charged across the valley and up the hill to where the wounded Hong Kong lay, when the whole party halted, and proceeded to butcher him in regular Indian style. After cutting out his heart, and other 'choice pieces,' they packed the remains off on a pole. The death of this man aroused the Hong Kongs, and they charged in turn, and drove the Cantons near a mile, but without being able to overtake them."

The latter group, however, appeared to still hold the advantage, which became apparent as the skirmishing continued over the next two hours or so. Finally, "the Hong Kongs, seeing they had a poor show with their spike poles against superior numbers, armed with muskets, drew off from the field in an orderly manner. The Cantons remained on the ground, and then drew off also."

It was only then, belatedly, that the deputy sheriff arrived at the head of a posse and started pursuing the withdrawing forces. He finally caught up to them about a mile down the road and began making arrests—at which point the combatants (presumably belonging to the Canton/Sam Yap group) turned on the posse and began firing. They got off about 40 shots in all, and while no one was hit, they provided enough of a distraction to allow all but one of the men who'd been arrested to escape.

Fortunately for the deputy, the one still detained spoke good English and was able to help round up the leaders. When all was said and done, four men were dead and 20 others had been injured, with the Yan Wo company having spent $20,000 in defeat and the Sam Yap group having shelled out twice as much.

All over a boulder that may or may not have contained a single gold nugget.

Promotional calendar from 1880 bearing stamps for
Chinese Camp and C.W.H. Solinsky.
Richard Beale collection

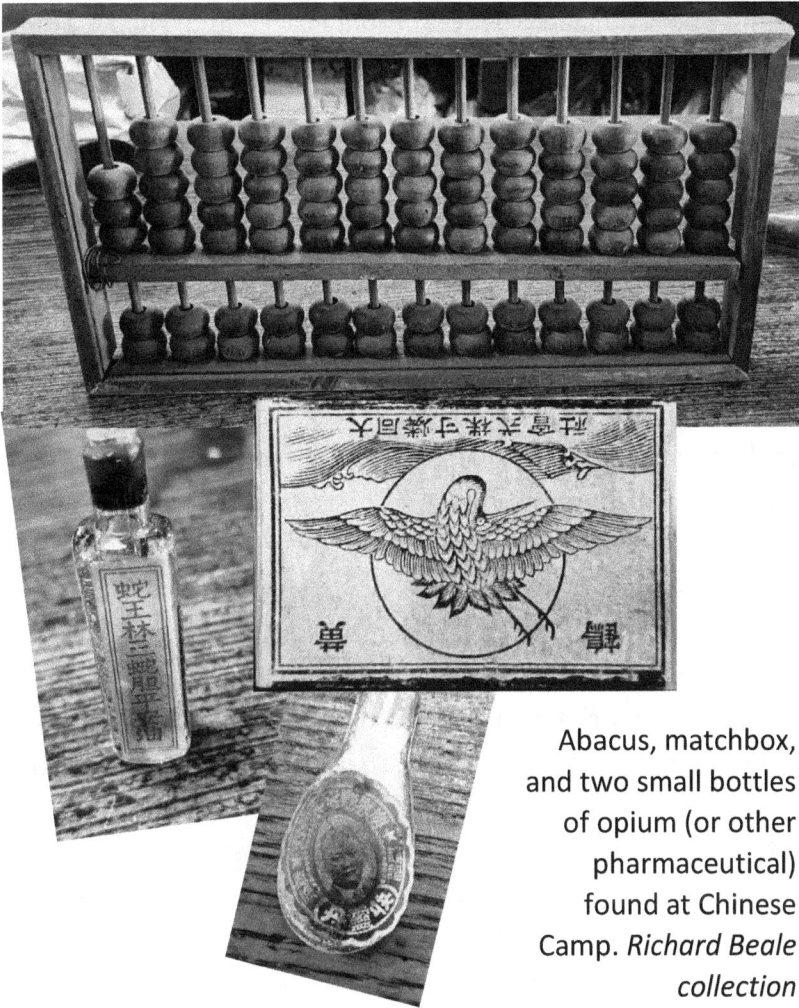

Abacus, matchbox, and two small bottles of opium (or other pharmaceutical) found at Chinese Camp. *Richard Beale collection*

Chinatown

The Chinese side of town has vanished today, but once upon a time, the "Chinatown" west of Webster Avenue constituted the greater part of Chinese Camp.

Chinese residents had their own businesses—either in buildings they owned or rented from white landlords—easily identified by wooden signs bearing the names of each establishment, clearly carved in Chinese letters.

"Hung Wo" translated as "Perpetual Peace," and Tuc Le Tong at the far end of Washington Street was a gambling hall euphemistically named the "Palace of Compound Interest."

By 1856, a total of 18 general merchants were operating in Chinatown, and 10 Chinese residents ran boardinghouses. Other businesses ran the gamut, indicating a fully functioning community. Of course there were saloons (three of them) and places where those in the know could find opium or female companionship.

But other Chinese businessmen provided a variety of services. Among them were seven doctors; six cooks and the same number of butchers; four bakers; and three seamstresses. There were also two barbers, two tailors, a pair of clerks, and a couple of grocers. Even a musician.

Town resident Saul Morris remembered the Chinese buildings as "mostly wooden with no floors, only earth." Residents of the district also, he said, had constructed "some very nice joss houses" (Chinese temples), that were "quite large, with very nice images."

While the white-steepled Catholic Church stood prominently on a hill overlooking the town to the east, Church Street wasn't anywhere near it: Instead, it ran north and south through Chinatown, where no fewer than three churches were listed as operating in 1872. The Hong Chee Church stood on the east side of the road, while the Man Chong and Ti, Ee churches occupied a large area of to the west, alongside a Chinese garden.

None of these, sadly, exists today.

By that time, some Chinese families had begun to take root, even as the overall population declined. In the early years, however, the vast majority of Chinese in town were men who had come there to work the mines. Even by 1860, the men still outnumbered the women more than 5-to-1, and children were even scarcer. The first Chinese child, a boy named Kwong Wo, was born in 1851. Nine years later, however, only two children, ages 6 and 3, were listed as living there.

Why so few families?

The Mother Lode was hardly the ideal place to raise a family. A few white women had come to town with husbands, but though they were outnumbered by the men, the numbers were even more unbalanced in the Chinese district. The Chinese women who did live there typically weren't married. In fact, 18 of them lived in one of three places—a boarding house and two saloons—giving every indication that they earned their living as ladies of the night.

While Chinatown occupied its own distinct area in town, it would be a mistake to suggest that the Chinese and white residents never mixed. The 1856 Kutchel and Dresel sketch of the Eagle Hotel, referred to earlier, shows a man on horseback and a horse-drawn carriage out front... along with the pigtailed figure of a Chinese man at the far right.

White residents often didn't refer to the Chinese by their given names, but by generic terms like "John Chinaman" and "China Mary." Where Chinese names were used, they were often preceded by "Ah," which—rather than being part of a name—was more akin to saying, "Hey, you there." Collectively, they were known, somewhat derisively, as Celestials, Chinee, or coolies (a generic term used for Asian unskilled laborers).

Such impersonal forms of address belied just how dependent the white residents were on their Chinese neighbors.

At one point, a Presbyterian minister, addressing the California Legislature, laid out the importance of immigrant patronage to businesses in Chinese Camp:

"There are four carpenter's shops where a number of mechanics are employed, at which they say upwards of one-half their business is from the Chinese. There are two livery stables in the township, both well supplied with horses, and paying well at present. The principal patrons, they say, are Chinese. There are two shoemakers' shops, of which the proprietors told me that seven-eighths of their trade are from the Chinese."

The writer referred to six American merchants, one of whom claimed that seven-eighths of his trade came from Chinese customers, with the other five putting the percentage at half or more.

"If it were not for the Chinese," he declared, "we would not have half our present stage coaches: More than half their receipts are from Chinese... They foster our trade, and consume our products, and at the present time there is scarce a man amongst us, from merchant to miner, that does not reap benefits either directly or indirectly from them."

On the other side of the coin, white residents ventured into Chinatown to purchase goods, partake of opium, find female companionship, and to gamble.

Something Up Their Sleeves

That Chinese and white miners were known to sit down together for a friendly (or not-so-friendly) game of cards is shown in Bret Harte's 1870 poem "Plain Language from Truthful James." More commonly titled "The Heathen Chinee," it was written as a satire of anti-Chinese attitudes in the Mother Lode, but was widely interpreted by racists as an excuse for condemning Chinese

Bret Harte

immigrants as deceitful and untrustworthy.

The setting is given as "Table Mountain," not far from Chinese Camp, and the poem concerns a game of euchre—a trick-taking card game played with a deck of 24 cards—that pitted a

Currier & Ives published this illustration of Bret Harte's poem "Plain Language from Truthful James" in 1871. The poem poked fun at a card sharp named Bill Nye who was outwitted by his opponent, Ah Sin, at a game of euchre. The clothing, shoes, and braided hair worn by Chinese Americans in this period are depicted fairly accurately. *Library of Congress*

card sharp by the name of Bill Nye against a Chinese man called Ah Sin.

In his opponent, Nye sees an easy mark: a naïve foreigner with a "pensive and child-like" smile who doesn't even understand the game... much less the fact that he is about to be cheated. Nye therefore resorts to his usual tactic of palming cards in an effort to guarantee victory:

> Yet the cards they were stocked
> In a way that I grieve
> And my feelings were shocked
> At the state of Nye's sleeve
> Which was stuffed full of aces and bowers
> And the same with intent to deceive

Above: Chinese Americans in traditional dress share a meal in San Francisco c. 1880. *Library of Congress*

Right: Portrait of a Chinese child. *Photo courtesy of Richard Beale, Chinese Camp Store*

That intent, however, is quickly thwarted by Ah Sin, who has, it turns out, been feigning ignorance about the game. Not only that, he's been hiding his own set (actually, multiple sets) of cards up his long sleeves—and using a sticky wax substance to first conceal, then retrieve them.

The narrator, also a participant in the game, may have been "shocked" at Nye's behavior, but he was equally nonplussed at Ah Sin's response—especially when the man happened to play one of the same exact cards the narrator himself was holding.

> But the hands that were played
> By that heathen Chinee,
> And the points that he made,
> Were quite frightful to see, —
> Till at last he put down a right bower,
> Which the same Nye had dealt unto me.

> Then I looked up at Nye,
> And he gazed upon me;
> And he rose with a sigh,
> And said, "Can this be?
> We are ruined by Chinese cheap labor," —
> And he went for that heathen Chinee.

> In the scene that ensued
> I did not take a hand,
> But the floor it was strewed
> Like the leaves on the strand
> With the cards that Ah Sin had been hiding,
> In the game "he did not understand."

> In his sleeves, which were long,
> He had twenty-four packs, —
> Which was coming it strong,

Yet I state but the facts;
And we found on his nails, which were taper,
What is frequent in tapers, — that's wax.

Harte's intention was for the reader to cheer that Ah Sin had given the devious Nye his comeuppance. Unfortunately, the writer appears to have overestimated the level of sympathy he could elicit from a white audience for one "heathen Chinee." The poem became wildly popular but, to the author's dismay, for all the wrong reasons: It was circulated as propaganda intended to clamp down on Chinese immigration leading up to the Chinese Exclusion Act. This legislation, signed by President Chester A. Arthur in 1882, placed a 10-year ban on Chinese laborers immigrating to the United States.

Chinese Exodus

At one point in time, unspecified by a later writer who only put it as "years ago" in 1924, a Chinese couple with four daughters lived in town. The father ensured they were well educated but passed before his daughters were of age, and his stern widow was left to look after them.

Such was their fame and beauty that suitors from as far away as San Francisco began to come calling. But these "rich merchants with all their silks and embroideries, seemed to fail to register in the hearts of the daughters."

Then a finely dressed man arrived there, of strong intellect and dignified stance, who was said to have been the emperor's tutor, and all the single girls in Chinatown turned out in their finest adornment to enchant him. The visitor, however, had come specifically to seek out one of the four daughters, who had been described to him as the "Eyes of Heaven."

Needless to say, the couple were soon wed.

A couple sits on the porch at Chinese Camp. *Photo courtesy of Richard Beale, Chinese Camp Store*

A second daughter was wed to a different suitor, a young engineer who would go on to help build the Panama Canal.

The third and fourth daughters' fates were not included in the account, but the writer concludes by referring to a series of smallpox epidemics that swept through town, claiming hundreds of victims who were buried in trenches.

The effects of disease, the gradual depletion of the ore that had drawn them here, and measures like the Chinese Exclusion

Act combined to make Chinese Camp less and less Chinese as the years wore on. This reflected a countywide decline: from 5 percent of the population in 1860 to 2 percent in 1880 and just 1 percent by 1920.

By the early 1900s, few Chinese residents remained in Chinese Camp itself.

In an apparent case of human trafficking, one Chinese girl named Yung Ida, who was born in the camp, was sold for $3,000 and taken to China by the person who had "purchased" her. Another woman, who'd come to town as a slave girl at the age of 11, was 85 years old when she finally left. Called "Duck Mary" because she raised ducks—many of which waddled along after her as she walked through town—she lamented having to return to China. But with no one to look after her in her old age, she was forced to leave with others who were returning to their homeland.

Still another man, Ah Chee, was well enough to remain behind in a small cabin on the knoll near the tiny Odd Fellows Cemetery. He was, however, addicted to opium... which was no longer available when his fellow Chinese immigrants left town for the Far East.

The town doctor, Daniel Stratton, took pity on him and sought to gradually wean him from the drug, doling it out to him in small quantities.

Most of the Chinese had departed by 1918, and the census of 1920 showed just two Chinese residents still in town: a middle-aged couple named Milly and Lum Sam Kee—known locally as "China Mary" and "China Sam"—living on Red Hill Road.

Two years later, they too were gone. Their departure was significant enough that it made headlines in the *Stockton Record*, which reported in its headlines that the couple were "going home after 65 years."

Sam had arrived in 1857, and "Mary" arrived shortly after that. At their impending departure, the *Record* declared they were "well known inhabitants of the Chinese Camp section" and "well thought of by the white residents who know them best. These will wish them a safe return to their native country."

At the time of the writing, Sam (then 81 years old) told the newspaper that there were still some 600 people of Chinese ancestry interred at an old Chinese graveyard "near the intersection of the Chinese-Montezuma road."

How many still lay there, and for how long, is unknown, but many were disinterred and their remains sent back to their ancestral land.

An early writer observed that, "while traveling in a desolate mountain region, I was much impressed by the sad, lonely form of a Chinaman, walking pensively toward a solitary grave, and scattering little papers as he went. These, it seemed, were his prayers to the spirit of his ancestors and the departed."

While no buildings from the Chinese section of Chinese Camp remain, you can find them in other Gold Rush towns, such as this building on Main Street in Columbia. Chinese shops such as this lined the road north of Jackson Street in the 1870s. *Author photo*

Top: The Sam Choy Store in Angels Camp was built in 1861 for Sam Choy (who ran a business there as early as 1856) and his partner, Yim Kee, and it remained under Chinese ownership into the 1890s.

Above: The "Stone House" brothel, built around 1865 in Placerville, is the last surviving building from that city's Chinese section. *Author photos*

New construction continued in Chinese Camp after the Gold Rush, but on a much smaller scale. This home on the northeast corner of Washington Street and Red Hill Road was built around 1890. It was one of the dozen or so oldest buildings to survive in town as of 2024, and the only one to feature Queen Anne detailing. *Author photo*

After the Boom

Fire and water were two keys to the ultimate fate of Chinese Camp.

The town had shown its resilience in rebuilding after the catastrophic blaze of 1856, and the new structures set in place were better able to resist the effects of the fires that were simply a fact of life on the western frontier. Unfortunately, the damage that was done in subsequent years proved to be more permanent. As the town's fortunes declined, there was less incentive to rebuild... and fewer residents to do the rebuilding.

Fire would burn through town in 1863 and five more times between 1870 and 1880. The fire of 1870 destroyed a good portion of the Chinese district, "on both sides of the street," and though some of it was rebuilt, much was lost. In 1880, a "disastrous fire" destroyed barns owned by Michael Wilson and James Morris, along with a lumberyard and Louis Egling's blacksmith shop—which suffered a total loss. He was forced to rebuild.

Even sturdier buildings in town could succumb to the intense heat of the fires that roared through town in those later years. One account, set down later, showed just how hot these blazes could get:

"A fire removed what would today be a very interesting ruin," an *Oakland Tribune* reporter wrote in 1924. "The old brick building still stands, a mere shell of its former self, for the fire which destroyed it was terrific, fed by 3000 pounds of good miners' bacon stored in the basement. Many barrels of oil, paints and olive oil helped raise the heat to the point where whole bolts of cloth were shot heavenward from four to five hundred feet, landing on other historic buildings and wiping them out of existence."

Chinese Camp's fortunes didn't dwindle all at once, though. The cumulative effect of the fires, anti-Chinese sentiment, disease, and diminishing gold—along with, most significantly, the town's waning importance as a stage stop with the coming of the automobile—all contributed to its gradual decline.

'The Bankrupt Count'

Water first came to town in the first half of the 1850s courtesy of ditches, and a Chinese Camp Water Company was active by 1860, when it was assessed $1,500 for "water works in Grey Gulch." Our friends Sol Miller and Count Solinsky held shares in the company.

Service improved gradually over the next decade or so, with the Iron Pipe Water Company spending $4,000 on a water pipe and ditch that ran from the east side of Woods Creek to company property on a hill behind the Chinese Camp schoolhouse, where a brick tank had been built by 1870.

There's no sign of the tank today, and the rudimentary water system was apparently allowed to fall into disrepair, leaving the town reliant on well water today. However extensive the system was, it apparently wasn't sufficient to guard against the numerous fires that hit town in the 1870s.

Solinsky's interests gradually extended beyond staging, banking, and water into other areas as well. He had married the former Mary Amelia Sprague in 1856, and though she passed away before their 10th anniversary, the couple had two sons, William and Frank, and a daughter, Maggie. (William and Maggie would remain in Chinese Camp—with Maggie marrying stage driver Thomas Jackson before moving to San Francisco—while Frank would become a noted attorney in San Andreas and onetime law partner of Lt. Gov. J.B. Reddick.)

By 1866, the Count was serving as secretary of the Sherman Black Hawk Joint Stock Company, which held its annual meetings at the Miller & Company offices in Chinese Camp.

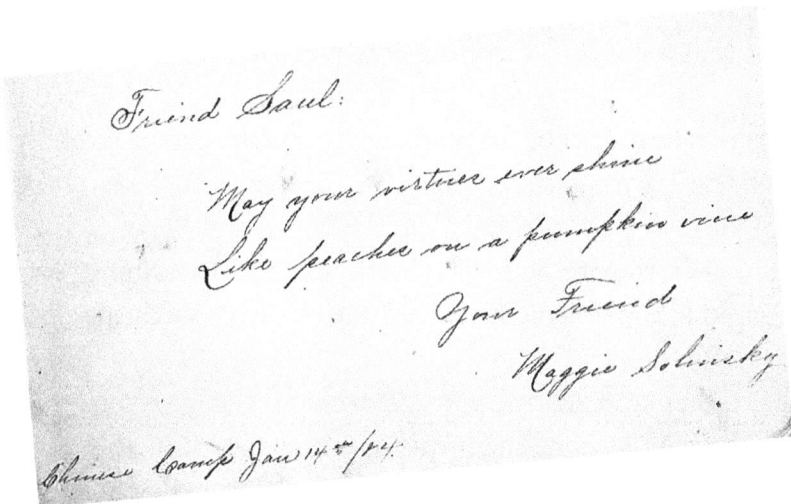

Maggie Solinsky penned this greeting dated Jan. 14, 1884, in "Friend Saul" Morris' autograph book. It reads: "May your virtue ever shine like peaches on a pumpkin vine." *Richard Beale collection*

Beyond this, he had gotten into the hospitality industry, purchasing the Garrett House Hotel sometime around 1863. It was a natural extension of his business running stages, providing travelers with not only transportation but a place to spend the night along the way.

Other hotels came and went over the years, including the Granite House on the west side of Webster south of Washington Street from 1860 to 1867 and the Lafayette next to Fred Weyer's brewery on South Main Street in 1865. Fred Ziegler owned a hotel in town in 1917, but it burned to the ground that year after a fire started in an adjacent shed.

The Garrett House, however, was the most famous and endured the longest. Its bricks, according to longtime resident Saul Morris' account, had been built of clay containing flecks of gold: Morris said those aware of this legend often took pen knives to the bricks, exploring for bits of treasure.

The hotel became even more popular under the Count's stewardship, housing what one writer described as "an embarrassingly large number of guests." So great was the demand for rooms that Solinsky used seven-foot partitions to divide them, thereby increasing the occupancy. One thing he wasn't able to do, however, was heat or cool the place, leading it to become so chilly in winter that it earned the unflattering nickname of "The Morgue."

In summer, the problem was the opposite, so the dining room was situated in the basement to keep patrons from sweating up a storm through dinner.

That didn't stop notable patrons from reserving a room for the night, though. Among them was Sir Thomas Lipton, the founder and namesake of Lipton Tea, whose favorite pastimes included yachting—his passion for which wasn't, however, sufficient to win a single America's Cup race in five attempts.

Other reputed guests included Ulysses S. Grant and, unsurprisingly, Mark Twain, whose presence seems to have been remembered in far more places than he could actually have visited. (A "Mark Twain cabin" along Highway 49 was actually built several years after his death.)

Solinsky was one of the first hoteliers in California to employ Chinese chefs. The staff at Garrett House under his ownership included a barber, a housemaid, two Chinese cooks, and a Chinese waiter. One of his sons worked the front desk as a clerk.

A later account remembered the Garrett House under his ownership as "an impressive, two-story brick building with iron shutter doors and windows. High ceiling rooms were darkened during the day to keep out the summer heat. Beds and feather mattresses... left the deep mould of a tourist's figure after the bed was remade."

Top: Mark Twain in 1884
Above: Thomas Lipton in 1909

The hotel had an "A" rating, one former guest recalled, but it may have gone downhill over the years, as stage traffic dwindled with the advent of railroads that gave travelers a more comfortable way to reach other destinations.

By the beginning of 1892, one writer was lamenting that Solinsky's once-thriving business was no longer drawing the throngs of patrons it had once attracted, referring to him as the "bankrupt count."

"One of the most interesting men characters in California," the writer began, "is Count Solynski [sic]who keeps an inn where refreshments may be had for man and beast at Chinese Camp, a rude little mining town in Tuolumne County."

The writer, somewhat condescendingly, referred to Solinsky as being "reduced to the position of one who serves" when he "started a hotel and got about him the miners, stage coach drivers and unhappy travelers who find they must pass through Chinese Camp"... as though to do so was some great burden.

His hotel, the writer allowed, was a success, albeit he contended that the Count was operating at a 1 percent loss on his investment. ("But as the Count had quite a sum of money when he started, he can continue losing the 1 per cent a year for some time.")

And despite his supposed financial woes, the writer painted a picture of Solinsky as one who continued about his duties with the kind of grace and good humor befitting one of noble birth.

Solinsky, he wrote, "is a man of great dignity, a perfect gentleman in an apron not over clean; a polished courtier to whom every man is a king; a philosopher to whom every one is a fool; an aged man whose years are as days."

A 77-year-old man who still spoke clearly without a tremor in his voice, Solinsky was given to caressing his "long white mustachio" as he spoke. Apparently having dispensed with much of the staff who had served at the hotel during the height of its popularity, Solinsky had apparently been reduced to a jack-of-all-trades who ran the hotel on his own:

"The Count waits on his guests himself; can cook and bake like the chief of some famous rotisserie; can brew liquors that would tempt a Kansas prohibitionist, and can ride anything from a bucking bronco to a stage coach."

The bar and dining area at the Garrett House. *Tuolumne County Historical Society*

The entire dispatch seemed an odd mix of pity and admiration for Solinsky, whom the writer seemingly saw as a long-suffering yet accomplished hotelier dedicated to serving those few patrons who still stopped to rent a room for the night.

It was not, apparently, a new situation.

Four years earlier, in the spring of 1888, another author painted this less-than-flattering picture of both Solinsky's establishment and the town as a whole. "We are to sleep at Chinese Camp," he wrote, adding that "the name is not attractive; and the town looked less so as we approached it."

The description that followed described the town in very much the sort of terms that would come to define it as a ghost town: eerie and dusty; unkempt and all but forgotten:

"A narrow, huddled street of low and dingy houses, set closely together as a city; a thick, hedge-like row of dwarfed locust trees stood on each side, making it dark and damp; many of the buildings were of stone, with huge studded iron shutters to both doors and windows of the first story; but stone and iron were alike cobwebbed and dusty, as if enemies had long since ceased to attack."

The writer had booked a room at the Garrett House, where he was greeted by the Count himself: "a middle-aged man, with the bearing and speech of a gentleman."

Solinsky was gracious in his welcome, declaring "I have not much I can give." But, he maintained, he knew the value of a clean room, and was aware of what travelers required on their journey.

The writer, like the one who would visit Solinsky four years later, seemed to pity the Count, being marooned, as he appeared to have been, in this town whose glory years had long since passed, apparently resigned to his fate as proprietor of a faded gem in the Mother Lode:

"His story is only the story of thousands of pioneers of '49. Glowing hopes, bitter disappointments, experiment after experiment, failure after failure; at last the keeper of a little tavern and the agent of an express company, he had settled down, no longer looking for fortune and success.

"There was something very pathetic in the quiet dignity with which he filled the uncongenial place, accepted the inevitable burden. His little daughter, twelve years old, had on her beautiful face a wistful look—the stamp of unconscious exile.

"'What will be the child's fate!' I said to myself as I watched her arranging with idle, lingering fingers a few bright wild flowers in an old pitcher. Who knows. There is promise of great beauty in her face and figure. Not the least of the exiled Count's griefs must be the anticipation of her future, in this wild, rough land.

"Perhaps," the writer mused, "she may yet live to be the landlady of the inn, and so perpetuate the cleanliness and good service which today make it memorable in the journey to Ahwahnee."

Sadly or otherwise, the writer's prediction did not come to pass. Solinsky's daughter did not become the inn's landlady. The

Count passed away in April of 1896 after a long illness, and the Fox family took over management of the Garrett House. The home belonging to the matriarch of that family, Elizabeth Fox, sat across Main Street from the hotel site before it was destroyed in the 2025 fire. Later a boarding house, it had been built around 1865 in Montezuma—which burned down the following year—and moved to Chinese Camp around 1905.

The Garrett House, unfortunately, does not survive, having long ago burned down. The livery stable associated with the hotel survived until 1901 but is also gone today. A narrow path called Solinsky Alley remains next to where the hotel once stood, its name a reminder of the Count and his family.

That Was Entertainment

Other thriving businesses from the halcyon days of Chinese Camp are gone as well. There were five saloons in town in 1862, and four were still operating in the mid-1870s. You can see the building that housed one of them—the A. Gross Saloon—on the northwest corner of Main Street and Red Hill Road. It was first noted in an 1873 assessment but had become a home to Samuel Wheelock by 1891. Wheelock still owned a saloon, but it was across the street.

There were other means of entertainment, too.

An early theater, long gone, operated in the 1850s where Curry Street intersects Red Hill Road today. Converted into an armory for the Civil War, it became home to a military company known as the Tuolumne Volunteers, under the command of one Captain W.H. Utter.

There was a one-mile racetrack and rodeo corral, too, on "a fine level stretch" just off Red Hill Road opposite the modern school building south of town. It was, one writer recalled, "the ideal place for a racetrack."

The A. Gross saloon at the northeast corner of Red Hill Road and Main Street. *Author photo*

"Money was readily subscribed, the track built and opened with a grand old barbecue. For many years it was a great Sunday attraction, then the mines began to peter out, the sports became broke, the track became furrowed by gopher and squirrel, a cigarette snipe, a fire, a grandstand gone, and now but a memory remains of what was at one time one of the best patronized race tracks in California."

A three-story brick building once housed Fred Weyer's brewery, one of the tallest structures in town, which ran the entire length of the block between Main and Washington streets. Born around 1830, Weyer owned land across Main Street from the brewery as well as behind the structure, across Washington Street. The father of four children he also served as a trustee for the Iron Pipe Water Company. He would eventually move to Oakdale and, later, Modesto, switching gears to became a hotel owner.

But in the 1860s and '70s, he owned the brewery. An ad for Levi Strauss once adorned one of its walls, recalling the days when Mr. Strauss—as a miner in the Southern district—took his overalls to a cobbler in Coulterville with a plea that he might keep them from ripping.

The cobbler's use of rivets did the trick... and helped pave the way for Strauss' new career making sturdy workwear for prospectors in the Gold Country.

Next door to the brewery stood a dance hall/brothel called Fandango Frank's, which one author recalled as being full of "cribs" and "fancy women." And next door to that, in turn, was the Robert Orford Store, built around 1856 and often referred to as the Fandango House itself.

(In 1870, Fandango House owner Frank Losano also owned land across the street that was home to an establishment called Meyer's Restaurant.)

Town Fathers

Stores came and went along Main Street and elsewhere.

Miller and Solinsky had their express office in a brick building near the lot now occupied by the Fox Boarding House.

An early mercantile called the Buck Store was run by T.B. Buck, who would form a partnership with E.E. Hedges in 1867 to create Hedges and Buck, a wholesale and retail grocer operating out of a two-story brick building at Main and Sutter streets in Stockton.

The Buck Store in Chinese Camp was housed in a white adobe brick building with iron-door shutters on Main Street. It no longer stands.

The Walkerley brothers, William and Martin, had begun operating a general store in a good-sized brick building by 1850 at the southwest corner of Main and Webster. A nephew, Martin Bacon, immigrated from England at the age of 17 and began running the place after the Civil War, also working as a banker and founding treasurer of the Yosemite Turnpike Road Company.

Bacon remained in town until 1876, when he left to sell stocks and bonds in San Francisco, after which the store was taken over by brothers Saul and Paul Morris.

Their parents, James (a Prussian immigrant born in 1825) and Pauline Morris, had founded a mercantile of their own in a large adobe building on Washington Street and started a family that included four sons and a daughter. Sometimes their place was classified as a grocery; other times as a dry goods store.

In 1862, the Morrises moved to Main Street, purchasing a brick building built by a Jewish merchant from Poland named Joseph Cohn a few years earlier. They operated their store there for the next few years, and it still stands, just northwest of where Main Street intersects Highway 49.

"Our store was typical of the times, with not much order and with mining supplies scattered about," Saul Morris would recall. "We carried everything from a needle to an anchor, even including fine imported china and glass from England, France and Bavaria.

"We prided ourselves on well-stocked shelves, often buying in carload lots which then had to be freighted from the railroad or from the Stockton boat levee. The books showed more than $250,000 in business."

After the brothers took over the Walkerley store at the other end of the block, Saul served as postmaster and ran a Wells Fargo Express office, along with a telegraph service. At some point in the 1890s, he repurchased the old Cohn-Morris store, which would also serve as the post office for many years. Morris' brother George worked out of the brothers' store, too, as a Wells Fargo agent...

Until he was murdered in a sensational killing on November 8, 1895.

Two men, Wesley and Albert McReynolds, were taken into custody in the case after their sister, Ada, came clean. Initially, it had been assumed that robbers had killed Morris in defense of cargo being shipped through Wells Fargo, but his brother Saul was unconvinced. A bag of money had arrived at the store by stage from Oakdale at midnight on the night of the murder.

If theft had been the motive, Saul Morris reasoned, why had the bag been left untouched?

With questions such as this in mind, he employed a detective by the name of J.W. Reilly (or Riley, spellings vary) from San Francisco to follow up on the suspicion that the McReynolds siblings were somehow involved.

With Reilly on the case, the truth began to emerge.

It was first discovered that the two McReynolds boys had been seen at the store just before the midnight stage arrived. It was then learned that, at one time, their sister Ada had been infatuated with George Morris, but her attentions had been rebuffed.

With this information in hand, the detective secretly situated himself underneath the brothers' house every night for two weeks, until he finally overheard what he believed to be an incriminating conversation. He then befriended Ada, pretending to be a life insurance agent with a $5,000 policy George Morris had made out—naming her as beneficiary. He then seduced her in the hope that she might confide in him, assuring her that the policy would only pay if it could be firmly established that he had met a foul end.

In the naïve hope of obtaining a big payout, Ada swore out a written statement declaring that her brothers had killed George Morris in revenge for spurning her advances.

If the brothers had made it *look* more like a robbery, they might just have gotten away with it. Stagecoach holdups, even at that relatively late date, were still known to occur. In fact, just a year earlier, a Wells Fargo express stage with five passengers on board was the victim of just such a holdup when traveling

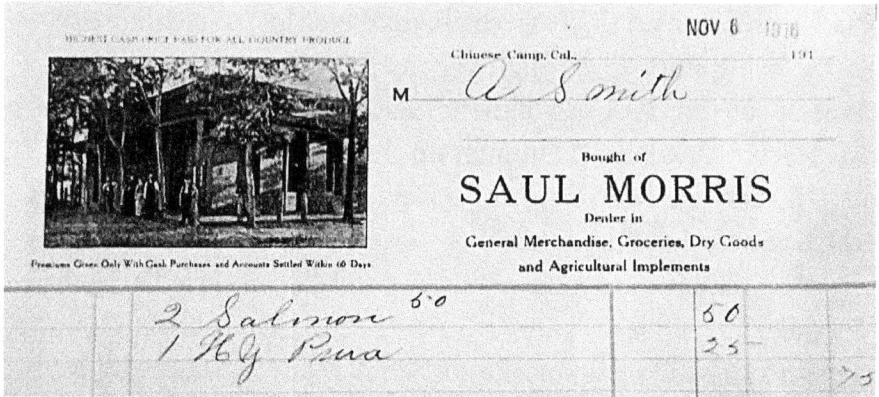

This 1916 receipt from the Saul Morris Store includes a photo of the establishment, which became the post office and still stands on Main Street near Highway 49. *Richard Beale collection*

from Oakdale to Knight's Ferry, Chinese Camp, and on to Sonora.

Paul Morris recounted the story nearly 50 years later in a story that appeared in the *Oakdale Leader*:

"It was one of those nice warm days of July, in 1894," he recalled. Andy Shine was driving one of John Shine's stages, with the U.S. mail and Wells Fargo bags occupying "quite a space in the stage."

Mail had been dropped off at Knight's Ferry and the small community of Cloudman, which had a post office back then, when he heard someone say "stop," at the top of Crimea Hill. "At first he thought the sound came from a chirping bird, and it was with astonishment he saw a man step from behind a clump of brush and heard him ask for one of the mail sacks."

The stage driver complied, and, "apparently satisfied, the bandit beat a hasty retreat toward Six Bit Gulch."

The driver and his passengers rode on to Chinese Camp, where they recounted their puzzlement that the bandit had asked for a mailbag instead of the Wells Fargo money box.

The Morris Store

"The general merchandise store at Chinese Camp of Saul Morris was established by his father in 1852. At his death the business descended to four sons, but it is now owned and conducted exclusively by Saul.

It is a fine establishment, carrying an immense stock of general supplies, all of which are selected with care. The store has a large patronage, people for miles around doing their trading at it. As a matter of fact, some residents of other towns deem it advisable to purchase at the store because of the uniformly fair prices, the superior quality of goods and the courteous attention accorded customers.

For the Morris store no order is too large, for the very simple reason that it can be filled; nor is any too small, for the similar reason that it will be given the same care as one of superlatively greater value; Mr. Morris insists that the purchaser of a five-cent spool of thread be accorded the same consideration as the person buying a thousand dollars worth of goods. It's his policy to treat all patrons alike..."

Tuolumne County, California, 1909

The sheriff and his deputy nonetheless picked up the bandit's trail, which led to a ranch—often left vacant by the owner—about three miles away.

They entered to find a man sitting there, unarmed and eating grapes, the unopened mailbag beside him. When questioned, he just started babbling, a vacant stare in his eyes. The sheriff was "quick to observe he had a maniac to deal with," and slipped a pair of handcuffs on him without a struggle.

He later discovered that the man had slipped away from an asylum in Sonora unnoticed—to which he was returned without any further fuss.

The Good Doctor

Saul Morris remained in town for many years after that, and was for a time known affectionately as "the mayor of Chinese Camp" (even though the town didn't have an actual mayor).

The Morris family apparently owned a two-story building that still stood on Main Street before it was lost in the 2025 fire, but Saul Morris' own home was dismantled and moved to Oakdale where it was converted into a pair of cottages around 1920.

He eventually moved to Stockton and outlived all his brothers, passing away in in 1953.

Another early postmaster of Chinese Camp was Charles B. Cutting, who had come to town from Massachusetts with his father Daniel, traveling across the isthmus of Panama to get there. They came for health reasons and stayed, liked so many others, to mine gold.

Daniel Cutting, unfortunately, died in February of 1867 amid what *The Sacramento Bee* called the most severe storm of the season. He was attempting to cross Six Bit Gulch with a two-horse team when he was swept away by the current. The horses, also caught in the water, drowned as well.

But Charles Cutting would settle down to the life of a businessman and a town leader, running a store and serving as a justice of the peace, postmaster, telegraph agent, and notary public in 1875. Like his fellow merchants, Martin Bacon and Count Solinsky, he was involved in the Yosemite Turnpike Road Company, which built the first road down from Tamarack Flat to the Yosemite Valley floor. Cutting was, in fact, the actual

One of the oldest homes in Chinese Camp, this house on Red Hill Road just north of Main Street was built around 1870 and once belonged to Charles Cutting. *Author photo*

paymaster for the construction crews on the project, and his family retained his records.

Postmaster duties would remain in Cutting's family for decades, with his wife assuming them in the early 1900s after his death, and his daughter Helen Stratton serving in the position for 15 years before retiring in 1949.

Helen had married Daniel Stratton, another fixture in Chinese Camp who had set up a medical practice in town. Their daughter, also named Helen (Stewart), carried the torch even further, running the post office until 1967.

Stratton, for his part, had come to town with the intention of visiting his sister, Rachael, who had married into another well-

This house east of 49 on Main Street served as Dr. Stratton's office. It was built around 1900 and may have been moved here. It was lost in the fire. *Author*

known pioneer family in the area: the Kerricks. She was, at the time, running the Crimea House that had been founded by James Wallace Kerrick, and had written to him about the natural beauty of Yosemite, urging him to pay her a visit and see it for himself.

Stratton was in his late twenties and had just completed medical school at Iowa State with the intent of starting his career at Boston General. But after accepting his sister's invitation to visit her in the Sierra foothills, he abandoned those plans and remained in California, never to return.

Why on Earth would a young surgeon with a promising career ahead of him exchange a life of urban excitement on the East Coast for a practice in a small frontier town out west?

It must have been love. For it was in Chinese Camp that Stratton met Helen Cutting, who was only 17 at the time but who, at her parents' urging, accepted his proposal of marriage. He purchased a home and practice belonging to the town's previous physician, Dr. Lampson, at the upper end of Main Street.

She gave birth to their first daughter, Viola, in 1890, and their second, Helen, in 1902. (Stratton must have really loved his wife, because the name Helen lived on in the family: Modern resident and family descendant Helen Lund described herself as one of "seven Helens" in the family.)

The Eagle-Shawmut Mine

As time passed, the era of individual claims faded and the age of large-scale mining began. The Eagle-Shawmut Mine, about 3 miles east of Chinese Camp, exemplified this large-scale approach to extracting ore from the ground.

Prospectors had searched for gold in the area starting in 1850, with the Eagle and Shawmut starting off as separate claims, and mines operated there until 1892 (when a 10-stamp mill stood on the site). They shut down for five years, then reopened in 1897 later under the auspices of the Eagle Shawmut Mining Company.

By 1915, the operation had grown substantially, featuring some 14 tunnels reaching depths of up to 3,124 feet. A 200-horsepower motor was used to extract ore from the earth with a 30-inch-wide belt that ran 120 feet down the hill from the mine. The site included a 100-stamp mill, with each stamp weighing 1,250 pounds, operating 100 times a minute.

The mine produced $7.4 million worth of ore, it was, in 1909, the largest mine in the county. A commentary on the mine in 1900 noted that "the Eagle-Shawmut ore is of very low grade," but added that "what it lacks in quality is made up in quantity," with 150,000 tons are put through the mill annually and a chlorination plant that treated 15 tons daily.

The mine operated until 1947, but construction of the second Don Pedro Dam put it under water. Shawmut Road, which once connected the town with the mine, disappears into the water at the lake's edge today. But you can still look across and see the mine's ruins in dry years.

Top, above: Two views of the mine before it was inundated by Lake Don Pedro. *Photo courtesy of Tuolumne County Historical Society*

Inset: Mine saloon token. Many saloons and brothels minted their own tokens to be redeemed in-house. *Richard Beale collection*

From top: Old miner's cabin moved to town from Eagle-Shawmut but lost in the 2025 fire; the shoreline where the mine is submerged; Shawmut Road now ends at Lake Don Pedro. *Author photos*

Stratton specialized in orthopedics but also had experience as a general physician, surgeon, pharmacist, and even a dentist, so he was able to see to all the community's needs. He not only made house calls around the area—with his wife accompanying him as a nurse/assistant all the way from Jacksonville to Yosemite—but he also served as the company doctor to some 250 workers at the Eagle-Shawmut Mine three miles east of town.

A 1909 publication touting Tuolumne County sang the praises of Dr. Stratton:

"When you need a physician, you need one badly, but a good one if possible. Chinese Camp has a good one—an excellent one—in the person of Dr. D.E. Stratton, who for years has controlled the practice of the western part of the County. He is also a skillful surgeon, having performed many successful operations, some of an extremely delicate and dangerous nature."

In his spare time, Stratton engaged in a variety of hobbies ranging from carpentry to beekeeping and photography. He trained horses, collected cars, and raised chickens. He even carved a clock from the center of a giant redwood in Yosemite, for which he won a prize at the World's Fair in San Francisco.

The Final Stages

Doctor Stratton's hobby of collecting cars pointed to a shift in transportation habits of Gold Country travelers. Saul Morris, similarly, was eager to get behind the wheel of a horseless carriage.

In 1912, he took delivery of a new automobile constructed by the E-M-F Company, which sold its cars through Studebaker wagon dealerships—owned by onetime Placerville wheelbarrow-maker John Studebaker. (Studebaker's company would take over E-M-F the following year.) To house his new prize roadster, Morris sent fellow Chinese Camp resident Robert Sims up to Jamestown for lumber to build a new garage.

Forrest Lumsden is seen driving one of his family's stages around the turn of the century. *Photo courtesy of Tuolumne County Historical Society*

Morris would stay in Chinese Camp for a few more years. But in June of 1919, he took delivery of a new Studebaker from Stockton, and a year later, he had sold his house and moved west himself to the Port City.

This turn of events showed how quickly things could change.

Morris himself had continued to run a stage line out of Chinese Camp, employing a driver named George Egling (the son of Louis Egling, whose wheelwright shop had been destroyed in that 1880 fire). As late as 1911, a short update from Egling in the *Stockton Evening Mail* reported that business was "good all along the line." But when cars were first granted access to Yosemite three years later, the Morris stage company saw the writing on the wall. It stopped running coaches up to Yosemite and added an announcement that their toll rate referred to automobiles and that their vehicles were "not used with horses."

Of course, people with cars of their own—and there were an increasing number—could simply drive themselves. And now that they could get to Yosemite on their own, business was bound to suffer.

So, not long after that, the business folded.

Top: The Daniel Stratton Barn on the north side of Main Street east of the highway, was built on the foundations of an earlier barn owned by Dr. Lampson around 1925.

Above: This small house on the opposite side of the road dates to about 1900 and is in such bad shape it looks more like a barn. Both these buildings were lost in the 2025 fire. *Author photos*

Heyday to Mayday

The era of the stagecoach had ended. It had survived, perhaps, longer than anyone might have predicted. The railroad had laid down the first challenge to the dominance of stage travel, with a line opening up at Milton in Calaveras County in 1871, running east from there through Copperopolis to Sonora.

But it wasn't until more than a quarter-century later, in 1897, that a railroad came through Chinese Camp. Actually, it stopped in an open field about a mile to the west, at a place called Chinese Station, but that was close enough. The Sierra Railway had laid track from Oakdale east to Don Pedro, then north from there through Chinese Camp and Montezuma to Jamestown. There, with great fanfare on November 10, a crowd of 5,000 people gathered to celebrate the line's completion with fireworks, dancing, and the driving of a golden spike.

The first "excursion train" from the "lower country" arrived shortly after the line was completed, bringing with it 500 passengers to partake in festivities that included a keynote speech, races, and a grand ball.

Paul Morris would later state that stage traffic between Big

TO THE PUBLIC.

Effective August 5th. The Sierra Railway Co. of Cal. will be prepared to handle both Freight and Passenger business to Don Pedro, a permanent station located one mile south of old Crimea Honse.

Teamsters are now charging $5.00 per ton on freight from Cooperstown to Sonora, Jamestown, Stent, Quartz Mountain, etc. From Don Pedro the charge will be to Sonora $3.50; to Stent, Quartz Mountain and Jamestown, $3.00 per ton. Freight consigned to mountain points via Cooperstown, on and after August 5th, will be carried forward and delivered to teams at Don Pedro.

Stages will meet all trains at Don Pedro for Chinese Camp, Jamestown, Sonora, Stent, Quartz Mountain, Shaw's Flat, Springfield, Columbia, Jeffersonville, Soulsbyville, Cherokee, Summerville, Confidence, Jacksonville, Groveland, Big Oak Flat, Tuttletown, Yosemite Valley and other mountain points.

B. T. Booze,
G. F. & P. A.

Oak Flat and Sonora "died out when the Sierra Railroad was constructed," and the blunt, somewhat sarcastic verdict of the *Union Democrat* in its 1909 publication *Tuolumne County, California*, reveals why:

"The people have discovered that quick traveling in commodious car beats the old fashioned, slow stage coaches, even if the erstwhile comforts of weariness, mud, dust, and an occasional hold-up by robbers can no longer be enjoyed.

"But in this connection, it should be remembered that the stages have not been relegated to oblivion; neither have the freighting outfits with their ten to sixteen animals. Both are still at work, but only from places not on the line of the railroad to the nearest station."

In fact, the Morris brothers operated their stage line for nearly two decades after the rails were laid. The railroad, after all, didn't go to Yosemite, and demand among tourists to experience the beauty of this high-country wonder (made a National Park just recently in 1890) was only growing.

"As a very young man, I was opposed to the railroad coming any closer because we all liked the teamsters and were afraid that they would lose their jobs," Saul Morris later confessed. However, he added, "It was a misconception. The closer the railroads came, the more work they had."

The Nevada Stage Company moved most of its stage drivers and coaches from the Silver State to California in the 1870s and established a "Yosemite Run" from Milton, with stops at Copperopolis and Chinese Camp. Tickets from San Francisco to Yosemite Valley on this line were $30. A separate staging service offered a line from Milton up through Angels Camp and Murphys to Big Trees for the same price.

A brief interview with C.O. Drew of the Nevada Stage Company with the *Stockton Evening Mail* in the late spring of 1888 revealed that conditions for travel to Yosemite were ideal, with the roads free of both dust and mud.

"Cold?" the reporter asked.

"Not enough so to be at all uncomfortable," Drew responded. "The ride through the mountains is simply delightful. There is greenness and freshness at every turn. Even the six inches of snow which fell and was lying at Crane's Flat when I came along will be all melted and out of sight—all run away—before I get back there."

The Yosemite stage service was purchased by the Great Sierra Stage Company and, after that, by Captain W.A. Nevillis, who rechristened it the Big Oak Flat Yosemite Stage Company. It got

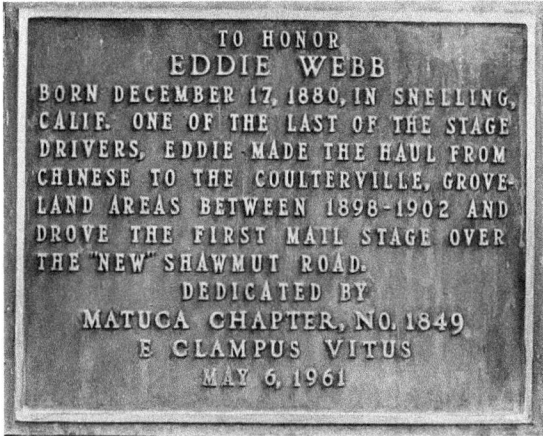

Plaque dedicated to Chinese Camp stage driver Eddie Webb by E Clampus Vitus in 1961, which appears on the Cohn-Morris Store/old post office. *Author photo*

another new name in 1899, when Chinese Camp resident Daniel Lumsden (who, with his brother, had carved a tunnel through the Dead Tree at Tuolumne Grove) bought it.

An announcement in the *Stockton Evening Mail* declared that daily service between Chinese Station and Yosemite would commence on May 15, with rides priced at $10 each way. You could expect to leave Chinese Camp at 4:40 p.m. and arrive in Yosemite Valley about 5 p.m. the following day "following a good night's rest at Priest's hotel." The return trip commenced at 8:30 a.m., with lunch at Crocker's—a waystation of 15 buildings completed around 1881 between the road and the South Fork of the Tuolumne River—and another night at Priest's.

Chinese Station today (author photo, top) and in its heyday, with the blacksmith shop that operated there (directly above). *Tuolumne County Historical Society*

Then it was back on the road at 5 a.m. so passengers could then arrive in time for the 8 a.m. train from Chinese Station to Stockton.

The Morris brothers bought Lumsden's business sometime around 1902 but kept Lumsden on as a driver and a partner. At one point, they also employed the services of a stage driver named Eddie Webb, whose service is commemorated with a plaque on the front of the old Cohn-Morris building.

At the age of 81, some six decades after he worked for the Morris brothers out of that very building, Webb still vividly recalled his days driving stages. He'd been interested in the profession since the age of 6, when his folks ran a hotel at Merced Falls (between Hornitos and Snelling, a little more than 30 miles south of Chinese Camp) that catered to stage drivers and their passengers.

After his father died, Webb—the eldest of seven children—became the breadwinner, driving his own freight wagon from the hotel to Coulterville, herding sheep and hogs over the 22-mile distance as well.

Webb was just 17 years old when he made it to Yosemite for the first time, driving an eight-passenger stage up from Coulterville in 1896, and shortly afterward started driving the graveyard stage from Coulterville to the new Chinese Station rail depot, leaving at 3 a.m. each morning to meet the 8 a.m. eastbound train departing from there. He'd stick around to pick up passengers from the westbound train after 4:30 p.m. and take them along with the mail freight south again to Coulterville.

When the afternoon train was late—as it frequently was—he might not get back to Coulterville until just before it was time to head north again at 3 a.m., meaning he had no time to get any sleep at all. (Unlike the afternoon train, the morning train was always on time.)

Considering this rigorous schedule, it's no surprise that Webb stopped working the overnight stage route in 1898 and went to work for the Morris brothers, driving the Yosemite Stage out of Chinese Camp over the Big Oak Flat Road.

On one occasion, he recalled pulling his five-horse, 15-passenger coach up in front of the Garrett House, waiting for his passengers' bags to be unloaded, then driving around the block to the stables directly behind the hotel, and finally spinning that bulky coach around in the middle of the street.

Another driver, Tom Hammond, saw him perform the feat and took up the challenge, declaring: "If Webb can turn around in the middle of the street, I can too."

As he undertook to duplicate Webb's exploits, Paul Morris came running out of the store and shouted, "The next driver to try this stunt will be fired on the spot!" (Both men, as far as we know, kept their jobs.)

The Garrett House was, naturally, a primary destination for the stage, being the premier—if not, by then, the only—hotel in town and being situated, as it was, almost directly opposite the Cohn-Morris building. Every day at noon, the cook there would press a buzzer to indicate the midday meal was ready, and a bell would be rung, alerting all the drivers and passengers to head for the dining room.

Once, however, someone mistakenly pressed the buzzer at 10 a.m., and the bell was rung in response for at least five minutes. The entire town gathered in front of the hotel to find out what all the ruckus was for.

The Way to Yosemite

In 1881, a new road into Yosemite Valley from Wawona was built using largely Chinese laborers, some of whom probably came from Chinese Camp. The impetus for this new road wasn't finding a way into the famed valley, but to a remote silver mine that had previously been accessible only by trail using pack animals.

The original prospectors didn't stick around long enough to cash in on their find, but two men from Boston, Gerald Gifford and Theo Barney, pulled into Chinese Camp shortly after that and paid a guide named Leo McAdams to take them to the site. They reported back to the Swift Brothers, wealthy meat packers from Chicago, who decided to invest in the project. They dug a 4,000-foot tunnel into the mountainside but needed a wagon road before they could begin operations.

They chose W.C. Priest as superintendent of the road, and he told them they could do the job with the least expense using Chinese laborers. Taking his advice, they formed a road crew of 250 Chinese workers—each of whom was paid $1.20 a day—and 90 white laborers, each of whom was paid 30 cents more.

James Lumsden, foreman on the project, started out making $1.75 a day and had his wage increased to $2 before the road was done.

Lumsden had come to California from Vermont via Panama in 1859 and settled in Chinese Camp—in time to vote for Abraham Lincoln in the following year's elections. David had already settled in town three years earlier.

"I bought a fourth interest in a mining claim at Chinese immediately after my arrival and worked it for two years," he recalled in a 1925 interview with the *Stockton Record*. "We had a carting claim: We had two dumpcarts, one drawn by a mule, the other by a horse, and we had to cart dirt a half-mile to water to wash in a sluice box."

The enterprise was an abject failure: James ended the two years $400 in arrears after taking out a loan from his brother, who had enjoyed more success in his own mining endeavors prior to James' arrival.

After he "threw up this claim in disgust," he went on to try their luck on Moccasin Creek, but couldn't even make money to pay his board. Finally, he went to work as a ranch hand and his steady income of $35 a week gave him enough income to repay the debt to his brother.

Somewhere around the time he was hired as foreman to help build Tioga Road, he became involved with another project in the same vicinity.

James Mason Hutchings and the toll road builders had come up with an idea for attracting tourists to the area: a tunnel or "driveway" through one of the trees in the Tuolumne Grove west of the valley.

Hutchings had a mixed history in Yosemite (then referred to as Yo Semite or Yo-Semite). He'd led the second tourist party to Yosemite in 1855, built his family home there, and had purchased the Upper Hotel for $400 in 1864, renaming it the Hutchings House.

Two months later, however, President Lincoln deeded Yosemite to the state of California in a grant that restricted settlement there. The administrators of the grant said Hutchings had no right to own the land they'd purchased and forced him to sign a lease to continue operating the hotel.

During this time, Hutchings hired John Muir to run his sawmill, but he became jealous of Muir's growing reputation and Muir quit two years after taking the job. Hutchings never mentioned him in his writings, but Muir spoke glowingly of Hutchings' daughter Flo, the first non-native child born in Yosemite Valley. The "little black-eyed witch of a girl" was, in his words, "a smart and mischievous topsy that can scarce be overdrawn."

Though he accepted the original lease, Hutchings fought back against what he considered the government's unlawful confiscation of his land. He took his case all the way to the Supreme Court, but lost there and finally left after refusing to accept another lease, instead taking a $24,000 buyout to quit the park in 1875.

He moved to San Francisco, and that might have been the end

Building the Road

The Great Sierra Wagon Road is rapidly approaching completion. Harry Medlicott's graders from this side have reached the upper end of Tuolumne Meadows, while Priest's pick and shovel brigade from the other side are on Rocky Canyon Creek, leaving a gap between of little more than three miles, all of which is easy grading.

Priest's powder gang, following the picks and shovels, reached Lake Tenaya Thursday and will skip the heavy blasting along the margin of the lake for the present and follow up to the Tuolumne River, after which one hundred blasters will be put on to finish the three-fourths of a mile along the lake.

It is believed that freight wagons will reach Tioga by or before the end of the month. The construction of this road was a stupendous and costly undertaking and the Eastern capitalists to whose enterprise and public spirit the people of this county and coast are indebted for a great thoroughfare to a hitherto inaccessible but rich and extensive region, deserve to be remembered with gratitude.

Homer Mining Index, Aug. 11, 1883

of his involvement had that state not, oddly, named him "Guardian of the Yosemite Grant" in April of 1880 (replacing Galen Clark, for whom Louis Egling built a wagon). He therefore returned with his family to his home there.

Upon his return, he took notice of the Tuolumne Grove of Giant Sequoias west of the valley along the Big Oak Flat Road and realized it offered an intriguing opportunity. In that grove stood a giant tree with a particularly broad base that Hutchings thought

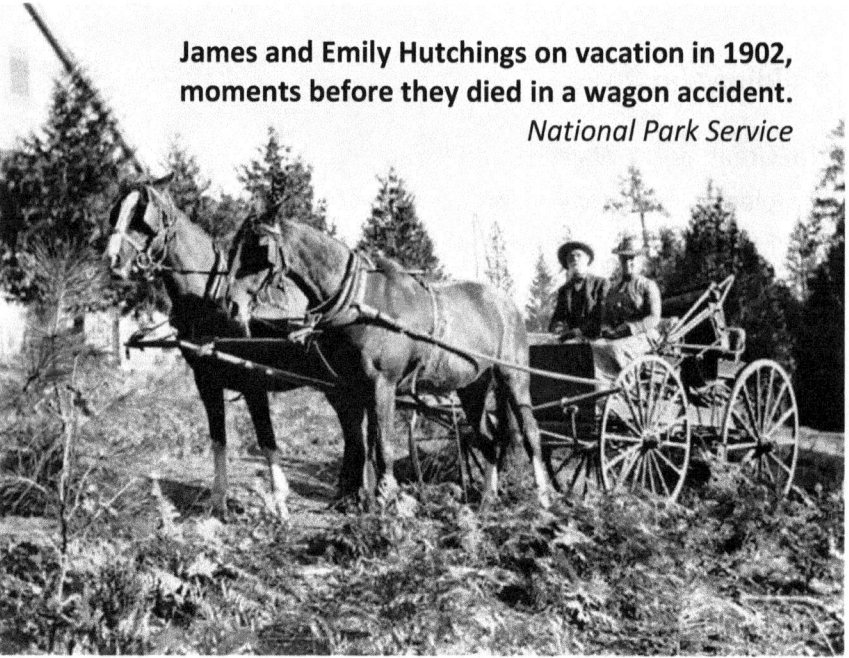

James and Emily Hutchings on vacation in 1902, moments before they died in a wagon accident.
National Park Service

would be perfect for a "driveway" through which stages could pass. Ever the promoter, he envisioned a tunnel through the so-called Dead Giant as the perfect tourist attraction—especially with the new road about to be built.

The toll road folks were all in favor of the idea and gave it the green light, so Lumsden and his brother put themselves up for the job. They bid $200 and got the contract.

"We worked 14 hours a day for 18 days cutting the tunnel," he said. "The tree was hollow, having been burnt out by fire, and we cut through from both sides. We used three-inch augers to cut the roof plane and chopped the rest out with axes."

But the $200 wasn't the end of their profit. They saved the wood from the tree, fashioned it into square and diamond shapes, and sold it to tourists who passed through on stages: "We chopped at the tunnel during the day and worked on souvenirs around the campfire at night. We had quite a pile of wood when we got through."

The Dead Giant tree in Tuolumne Grove. *Brian Grogan, Historical American Engineering Record, Library of Congress*

As for the toll road, the crews needed just 130 days to complete it "without interruption or accident." Road work was suspended before the coming of winter 1882 and resumed the following April.

The project was completed at a cost of $62,500, and excitement was high concerning the rich vein of silver that was about to be mined. The road allowed the delivery of heavy machinery and supplies to the site, where a sawmill had been built to facilitate the construction of buildings.

Then, one day, after spending $250,000 on the project in

addition to the cost of the road, the Swift brothers simply pulled the plug.

The miners wanted to keep working, but the air pipes were removed, making the air inside unbreathable. So the machinery was abandoned and left to rust, and the road became blocked by overgrowth until the government purchased it in 1915 and finished it, crossing the Sierra all the way to Mono Lake.

A tollgate keeper stands outside the booth on the South Fork of the Tuolumne River. The sign includes prices for all sorts of transportation methods livestock to both Yosemite and Crocker's. It would cost you $1 a person whether you were traveling to Yosemite by stage, automobile, on horseback, or by some other vehicle. Going in on foot or by bicycle would cost you 50 cents. *National Park Service*

Photos of unidentified subjects from the 18th century found in Chinese Camp. *Photos courtesy of Richard Beale, Chinese Camp Store*

Ghost Town Ghosts

What's a ghost town without a ghost or two, right?

Plenty of people stop by Chinese Camp today and swear they see shadowy figures in the windows of town, flitting away in the same moment they're discovered.

Then there are the graveyards.

One might expect a town this small to have one cemetery, but Chinese Camp has three—and that's not counting the Chinese Cemetery that once existed near the 49/120 junction from which so many Chinese immigrants were exhumed and returned to their ancestral homeland.

The City Cemetery was established up the hill right across the road from the Chinese Camp Store, and the Catholic Cemetery at St. Xavier's is adjacent to the church. The third graveyard was a very small IOOF plot on a knoll beside the highway on the east side, south of Main Street.

If you look carefully, you may spot the graves of some prominent former residents at the first two sites.

Gravestone of Patrick Quinn, who died in 1883, at St. Xavier's Catholic Church. *Author photo*

Tombstones at St. Xavier's Catholic Church, above and left, and at the small Odd Fellows Cemetery along Highway 49. *Author photos*

Gravesites at the City Cemetery, yet another site hit by the 2025 fire.
Author photos

Peacocks such as this one could be found roaming the streets and yards of Chinese Camp before the fire, and at least a few remain. More than a century and a half ago, a doctor named J.C. Peacock owned a hotel where the great fire of 1856 started... doubtless eliciting screams of terror not unlike the eerie calls of these colorful birds. *Author photo*

Paul Dale Roberts, an author and journalist who has been involved in more than 2,500 paranormal investigations since 2004 at sites including Area 51, the Paris catacombs, and the Tower of London, led a team of 17 investigators, psychics, and others, including a Spanish interpreter, on a visit to Chinese Camp in 2013.

Roberts, co-owner of Halo Paranormal Investigations, is also the Northern California location scout for the popular television show *Ghost Adventures*. (The site was not featured on the program, he explained, because he was unable to obtain permission from the landowner of one site to have the show investigate there.)

Paul Dale Roberts provided this photo of Joaquin Murrieta. He said psychic medium Deanna Jaxine Stinton identified the man in this picture as the figure she saw walking on the side of the road in Chinese Camp.

Roberts and his team investigated the Fox Boarding House; old post office; a barn; the city and Catholic cemeteries; and Dr. Stratton's property, including the old IOOF hall. Upon entering each of the structures—which had dead wiring and therefore no electricity—they received multiple "hits" on their K2 electromagnetic field meter, or EMF, a device that detects very low-range radio frequencies where spirit activity is believed to manifest.

Three K2 meters went off at once when certain questions were asked. Exploring in the Stratton property, Roberts asked, "Dr. Stratton, do you want to talk to us?" In response, he reported hearing an electronic voice phenomenon, or EVP, that stated, "Don't want to talk to you."

This photo taken in Chinese Camp in 2013 shows what appears to be the figure of a child standing on a rock at the extreme upper right. *Photo courtesy of Paul Dale Roberts*

Other EVPs were reported by team members at the post office ("My name is Tom") and the cemetery that says, "Paul, I'm in the ground."

"With all the EVPs we captured, I would definitely say that this place is haunted, and from a number between 1 and 10, 10 being the highest, a 12!" Roberts said. "There were investigators that told me later they felt like they were being touched. One walked through an area, and it went from hot to cold.

Roberts said his wife, psychic medium Deanna Jaxine Stinton, "saw the spirit of a man that looked like Joaquin Murrieta. The ghostly figure was walking on the side of the road and vanished."

Another photo, taken by a team member, shows what appears to be the shadowy figure of a child in the upper right-hand corner. Roberts believes the photo was taken near the church cemetery, which was right across the street from the old schoolhouse consumed by fire in 2006.

Could the figure be the ghost of a child who once attended there?

There are stories of other eerie encounters as well. Richard Beale, owner of the Chinese Camp store, tells a story of one local resident who claimed the devil appeared to him in the IOOF building.

He later overheard the same person say, "And then they made snow cones out of blood."

Who "they" were is unclear.

Whatever credence you give to modern reports of hauntings and paranormal activity, there's no doubt that the old IOOF, the Fox Boarding House, and other buildings in town seem eerie enough to make you look twice at changes in the shadows and stop in your tracks at an unexpected noise—especially at twilight or on an overcast day.

And it's equally true that Chinese Camp certainly has been home to its share of colorful characters who might haunt the town today, if one believes in such spectral sightings.

Helen Lund, a descendant of the good doctor Stratton and Charles Cutting, tells of a woman who used to spend the day sitting in an outhouse, watching the town folk as they walked past and went about their business.

There were, she said, seven saloons and two or three brothels in town, so it could be a rowdy place. And if you worked out in the Eagle-Shawmut Mine, you didn't even need to come back into town for some female "company": Lund tells of a cave out at the mine with a curtain that could be drawn across it. Behind that curtain, ladies of the evening would sell their "services" to men who couldn't wait to get back to Frank's Fandango House for some personal attention.

The saloons were busy, too.

"A Very Active Place"

As an experienced paranormal investigator in my free time, I have learned to get a feel for a place. I would never claim to be a sensitive, but there is a feeling one gets in a place that time may have forgotten, but its former inhabitants have not. I have done investigations in extremely active places like the Washoe Club and the Gold Hill Hotel in Virginia City, Nevada, as well as an abandoned asylum and in a home that was the site of a horrific murder of a family in Iowa.

While I did not get to do an investigation in Chinese Camp, I have no doubt that it is a very active place. I could feel the energy surrounding me as I walked down Main Street. It felt like if I looked around a corner, I just might see a stage rumbling down the road or a miner heading down to the saloon.

As an author of short stories that focus on horror, the paranormal and the supernatural, I was inspired to write a story set in Chinese Camp, so the people and the town itself would not be forgotten and just be relegated to pages in a history book.

Sharon Marie Provost

"Drunks would come up from the mine and fall over drunk in the street," Lund said, adding that they'd just lie there, and pedestrians would have to step over them while they slept it off.

Any one of these people would have made spirited specters in the afterlife, not to mention the numerous men shot, and accused outlaws hanged by vigilantes during the town's rough and bawdy formative years.

One such victim was a man named Dick Williams, whose ghost was said to haunt Chinese Camp in the 1950s. A newspaper account described him as "a hard working young fellow who left his family in the East and headed West with high hopes" but who "succeeded only in being strung up as high as his hopes had been."

Williams left his wife and two children at their farmhouse in Massachusetts and went off to seek his fortune, hoping to strike it rich and ensure a fine future for his family. On his way west, as chance would have it, he joined up with a fellow named Charley Moore, and the two agreed to share a claim.

At first, it seemed like a stroke of good fortune. The claim proved to be profitable, and after one particularly successful night, the partners went out for a night on the town to celebrate. Charley eventually left the saloon around midnight, but Dick stayed behind a little longer before he "weaved down the rough path to the tent the two shared."

A few minutes after Dick left the saloon, the miners still drinking there heard the sound of a shot being fired. They hurried to the partners' tent, lit a candle, and entered... to find Dick holding a gun, standing over the prone body of his partner lying on a bunk, a wet and growing bloodstain seeping through his shirt.

Dick, still clearly drunk, sputtered, "I didn't mean to shoot him. I thought I saw someone in here, so I just fired away."

Seeing the skeptical looks on the miners' faces, he lamented that, if they strung him up, he would leave behind a wife and two children who depended on him. They'd be left penniless with no one to look after them, and they shouldn't be penalized for what he insisted had been an accident.

He might have swayed them with this argument... if he hadn't kept talking.

"If you must hang me up, will you promise to send my wife my share of the gold Charley and I found?" he begged.

But that only solidified in his accusers' minds that it *hadn't* been an accident: that Dick had killed his partner in cold blood for greed and for gold. At sunrise, they hauled him off to a hanging tree and executed his punishment, then went back and retrieved Charley's body for burial.

It was only then that they discovered Charley hadn't been shot at all. He had been stabbed through the heart with a long knife, and no bullet was found near the body. Apparently, Dick had been telling the truth all along: He *had*, in fact, fired at an intruder intent on robbing them, but in his drunken state mistakenly believed he had shot Charley.

A posse went after the real killer, but he was never found.

And the ghost of Dick Williams was left to walk the streets of Chinese Camp, searching for the justice denied him in life and lamenting that he would never again see the wife and two children he'd left back in Massachusetts.

The Peek-a-Boo Ghost

Even in 1901, Chinese Camp was still described as a "lively little town," even though the Morris Brothers' store ("where miners could be outfitted from a needle to a haystack") was the only one still open. Indeed, it would remain among the county's seven most prominent communities as late as 1913—the year before the stages stopped running. But there was at least some evidence, as early as 1904, that it was becoming a ghost town.

Literally.

The ghost of Chinese Camp first made its appearance in June of 1904, about midnight (fittingly) in a stand of fig trees a block off Main Street. The streets were, as is natural at that hour, deserted except for a well-known photographer named A.C. Beck who had stayed up late with a friend developing plates.

Beck and his friend looked up to see what appeared to be a tall black figure walking down the deserted street. As they watched, however, it suddenly began to "glide away."

"Must be someone that's been for the doctor," one of the men remarked.

But then it happened again, a few nights later.

"Why, Al," the photographer's friend remarked, "that's the same thing we saw the other night."

And that was far from the end of it. From there, the ghost began making appearances all over town at all times of the night, not discriminating between drunk and sober residents; between those of good character and ill repute.

Miners appeared more likely than most to see the apparition: Their shift changes occurred at 11 p.m. and 7 a.m., making a confrontation with the spirit—which often seemed to show itself around midnight—all the more likely.

A man named Frank Crangle working the graveyard shift at the Shawmut Mine outside town saw it: a tall figure with a white veil over its face, descending from the hills and standing motionless in front of "the Leahy place." On that occasion, he dismissed it as someone out late, waiting to meet someone. But when it reappeared in the same place and manner the next night, he dropped to the ground and lay there prone until it passed... or simply vanished. Crangle couldn't say, but when he looked again, it was gone.

Three drunks from the Shawmut Mine came upon it next near the graveyard outside the Catholic Church overlooking the town, just above the home of Dr. Stratton. Another town resident, Jimmie Smith, saw it standing at the physician's gate and went to fetch reinforcements. But by the time they returned, the "apparition" had vanished again.

It was at this point that Stratton decided to take matters into his own hands. There was no doubt that someone or something had been unlatching his gate, running across his lawn, and disturbing his garden. Presumably that same someone had also thrown open the church's front doors and made a mess of things

Dr. Daniel Stratton's home and office, which burned down in 1920, were just east of Highway 49 and Main Street. He rigged a trap for the ghost, but it got away. *Photo courtesy Richard Beale, Chinese Camp Store*

inside the sanctuary.

Stratton therefore decided to rig up a "ghost alarm" by tying one end of a wire to his gate and the other end to the back of a large rocking chair in his sleeping quarters. It worked like a charm... except for one thing: When the rocker started thumping loudly against the floorboards, the good doctor slept right through it. His wife did hear the commotion but was so frozen with terror she dared not go out to investigate, and by the time she had awakened her husband, the interloper had fled into the night.

Archie McClain, who worked for the Big Oak Flat Stage Company, thought it strange that horses tied to their feeding stalls were found repeatedly separated from their halters... and some foreign object seemed to be responsible. So he kept watch one evening and, hearing a commotion among the horses, came upon the "real live ghost."

Of course, he was unable to capture it.

An employee at the Morris Brothers' store, H.C. Lot, was sitting outside after closing one night when he saw the figure—dressed in white and wearing a white mask—cross Main Street and turn down the lane behind Walsh's Saloon. George Egling saw it, too, as did Paul Morris, who nearly ran straight into it, but none of them deigned to confront it, and by the time they had gone to seek backup, it had disappeared.

Who Could it Be?

By this time, speculation as to the ghost's identity was running rampant. The favorite suspect appeared to be a fellow named Lim Phoon, described in one account as "a peaceable Chinese [resident], who came to an untimely end away back in the sixties..."

"As to the reason for his arising after so many quiet years spent below ground," the story continues, "they point to the fact that late last spring, an old Mexican murderer, released from San Quentin after a long term, came through Chinese Camp, traversing the scene of his early misdoings. He, it is suggested, aroused the spook."

Others were convinced it was a woman: Having seen it run away, they contended that "not even old Lim Phoon himself could swing his legs so wildly in a race."

Whomever the spook might be, it wasn't content to rest on its laurels, continuing to disrupt the town by climbing over backyard fences and appearing outside windows—most commonly pressing its spectral face up against the glass on occasions when women and children had been left alone.

Even those not afflicted by its visitations were loath to look outside at night, for fear they might find "a ghastly white face with horns" gazing back at them. Some residents stayed inside and avoided looking at windows, but others took a more proactive approach.

The Morris Brothers—who themselves had experienced a close brush with whatever-it-was—reaped a certain benefit from those who doubted it was a ghost... or, if it was, were convinced that it could be killed a second time. They quickly sold their store's entire inventory of guns, forcing them to put in a rush order for more firearms to a gun dealer in San Francisco.

Even men who'd never gone out "packing" were carrying guns and stocking up on ammunition. Many stood vigil, armed and at the ready. If it *was* a ghost, they reasoned, they'd make certain of that fact by shooting it and giving it a good laugh. But if it howled in pain instead of in menace, they'd know it was just someone out to scare the town folk.

Armed vigilantes had, not that long ago, been nearly a fixture around Chinese Camp. But with the Gold Rush now past, the community had become more sedate and the West a lot less wild. Perhaps the perpetrator of the modern "hauntings" had been counting on this, and now found the tables turned: They now had reason to be frightened.

Because the ghostly appearances suddenly stopped.

Everything seemed to be returning to normal when the community decided to throw a dance in the Eagles Hall at the heart of town. (This same building had once been used as a fandango hall, and over the years served as an opera house, casino, and Miners' Union Hall; it's gone today.)

One of the town folk, Nelson Williams, arrived to find music coming from inside and lights shining brightly from every window. But before he could cross the threshold, he came upon an odd figure dressed in fine attire and... a mask! At first glance, he assumed it was just one of the dancers, but a closer look at the mask revealed that it was nothing more than a black piece of material, drawn down over the face like a pall over a casket. The effect it produced made one feel as if they were staring at a corpse.

"Who in thunder are you?" Wilson demanded.

He then rushed inside to call forth the revelers as witnesses, only to find the figure had disappeared.

The Ghost Unmasked?

In the end, however, it wasn't guns but tubas and trombones that finally may have (indirectly at least) rooted out the "ghost." The instruments in question belonged to a 16-piece brass band just recently organized by William Haigh. They were known to practice late into the evening every Thursday night at the Eagles Hall. They locked the doors behind them when they departed, but one of the members—Spencer Shepard—happened to return around midnight to find the front door standing opened.

He rushed to close it, but before he could do so, he happened to glance through to the rear of the hall and see stars gleaming back at him... through the also-wide-open backdoor. Dutifully stepping inside to close the rear door before he exited again out the front, he was confronted by none other than the spooky white figure that had terrorized the town. At least he assumed it to be the same one.

And it was standing not three feet away!

The two having thoroughly startled one another, the figure ran for the back door and Shepard bolted out the front, making his way post haste to the nearest saloon and alerting the late-night drinkers there as to what he had seen. They all returned to find the "ghost" had vanished—but had left evidence of its frenzied departure in the form of overturned chairs at the center of the hall.

Again the specter had eluded capture, but not without leaving further apparent evidence of its presence... though it wasn't discovered until two days after the fact. On arriving to tidy

The Eagles Hall, which stood just east of the Garrett House Hotel, wasn't as grand as its name suggested.
Photo courtesy of Tuolumne County Historical Society

up the hall for a Saturday night dance, volunteers came upon blood in a small pool and splatters near the center of the hall, where the ghost had last been seen. The blood was dried and appeared to be about two days old.

Perhaps now, at long last, the mystery could be solved.

The query was then carried throughout town: "Is anyone in town suffering from a cut or injury?"

As it turned out, someone was: A certain woman had been under treatment for a gash on her head since the morning after the brass band's practice session at Eagle Hall. She reported having gone out that evening in search of her horse, which had escaped, and had ultimately collapsed from exhaustion. When she awoke, she found herself in front of bandleader Haigh's house with a cut on her head from a stone lying beside her.

Had this same woman, affected by pain and exhaustion, gone sleepwalking in the night and wound up at Eagle Hall? If so, how

---

STEPHEN H. PROVOST

had she entered through the locked door? Or was it all just a coincidence that didn't quite add up, and was old Lim Phoon or some other spirit still out there stalking the town?

A front-page story in the *San Francisco Chronicle* that year didn't provide the answers, and I couldn't find a follow-up story in that publication.

Almost three decades later, however, a story in the *Stockton Record* by none other than Paul Morris purported to solve the mystery. The *Chronicle* had said the whole ghost business started with a photographer, and according to Morris, it ended the same way: Once again, a local photographer was up late developing pictures when the ghost appeared. The man was distracted by his bird dog barking. Whether this was the same photographer or not isn't mentioned, but if it was, one can certainly imagine he'd had enough of all this nonsense.

He rushed to the front door of his studio and saw a figure running outside.

He went after it.

He picked up a rock.

He threw it...

Bull's eye!

He heard the sound of a crack, but the figure was able to escape once again. Was the rock found by the woman's head after the disturbance at the Eagles Hall the same one thrown by the photographer? According to Morris, when Dr. Stratton went to the woman's house to check her injury, he noticed khaki breeches—the sort the "ghost" had reportedly been seen wearing —in her home... And something even more incriminating: a white pillow case with openings cut into it for two eyes, a nose, and a mouth. Morris described Dr. Stratton's patient as "an eccentric woman, long a resident of the camp." After Stratton treated her, he said, "Chinese Camp's ghost was seen no more."

144

The Chinese Camp Brass Band, seen in the very year of the haunting. *Tuolumne County Historical Society*

Postscript (Ghostscript)

Chinese Camp resident Helen Lund named the woman in question as Alice Hopkinson, and indeed, a woman by that name *was* born in Chinese camp around the time of the Tong war and continued to live there for the rest of her life.

The woman's mother was so impressed by the Chinese shields used in that battle that she procured one to use for herself... as a crib for her newborn daughter. Alice kept that shield and hung it on the wall of her childhood home, described in 1924 as the second-oldest house in Chinese Camp, where she lived the rest of her life.

A story in the *Fresno Republican* recounted how the house had been hauled to its new location from 12 miles away by Alice's father, Morton Currie or Curry. (There's still a Curry Street in Chinese Camp today.)

"When the gold strike was made at Chinese Camp, knowing

the difficulty of procuring materials and workmen, Mr. Currie, instead of making any effort to build a new house, just hauled his ranch house to the strike and placed it neatly beside another house, just recently built in the camp."

But even if the woman wasn't a real ghost back in 1904, that doesn't mean she isn't one now. According to Lund, people around town have continued to see a face at the window which, they contend, belongs to the eternally curious woman who haunted them while she was still alive.

"She used to go around and poke her head into people's houses," Lund said. "We lived in her house with these old windows, and I swear to God, there were more people who said they saw someone looking in their window!"

The Chinese Camp Store & Tavern has been in business since 1934.

Before it Burned

While many of the town's leading citizens were passing on or leaving town, the Stratton family chose to stick around—even after the doctor's home burned down.

They sent both their daughters away to receive a higher education in San Jose.

Their eldest daughter, Viola, grew up to become a teacher at the Chinese Camp school she'd attended as a girl. Succeeding Dan Williams, who later became a state assemblyman, she started out making $200 a semester in 1910 when she took an assignment at the age of 19 in the one-room grammar school.

Though she never had kids of her own, she viewed the schoolchildren in town who attended the little one-room schoolhouse as her own.

By the time she retired in 1958, a lot had changed in the community: "I can remember when the town had a band, a baseball team, a general merchandise store and, of course, several saloons and two dance halls."

Viola Stratton Prothero still lived in town then, with her mother and sister Helen, at the family home: the former Oddfellows Hall at the corner of Main Street and Highway 49. It had been used by the Masons and the Knights of Pythias, too, before Dr. Stratton and his family moved there in 1920. The move had been necessitated by a fire that started in the washroom and destroyed his first home (along with all his surgical instruments) on the opposite side of the highway.

Other buildings from the Stratton property survive on the east side of 49, including a long barn built around 1925 and the doctor's former office: a small light-blue home across Main Street. A small hall-and-parlor house with the look of a barn, dating from around 1900, stands nearby.

The property where the Stratton home used to stand is now the site of several old miners' cabins hauled up from the Eagle-Shawmut Mine and other rickety wooden buildings. All that's left of the original home is the doctor's safe, which has sunk into the ground.

The mine is gone now too, submerged under the waters of Lake Don Pedro except in dry seasons when the water level falls so low that what's left of the old buildings is exposed. You can take Shawmut Road down to the water's edge, where the asphalt disappears under the surface, and look across at the mine site to see whether anything's visible.

"The man who located the Eagle-Shawmut Mine was a friend

Modern Chinese Camp school with a closeup of the new bell. *Author photos*

of my grandfather," Prothero recalled in 1977. "He went back to Minnesota and became a millionaire—timber, I think. His name was Musser. His daughter was here to visit me twice; I hear from her at Christmas... except the last year or two."

The old school where Prothero once taught outlived her but burned down in 2006. It hadn't been in use for more than 35 years but still sat up on a hill overlooking the town, across from the historic Catholic church. The new school, built in distinctive Mandarin style in 1971, was on 7.5 acres of land Prothero and her sister traded for the old school.

That trade, however, was not without controversy.

The school thought the old school bell was part of the deal, but the sisters disagreed, leading to a dispute that ended

This schoolhouse at top, shown around 1890, went up in 1852, but classes weren't held there back then. It started out as a boarding house for miners and later served as a church before finally being converted into a school. The new building, seen above around 1930, replaced it in 1906. *Tuolumne County Historical Society (top); University of Southern California Libraries*

A panorama showing the school when it was relatively new. Note the clean paint job on walls and trim compared with the weathered look on the previous page. *Tuolumne County Historical Society*

with the original bell's disappearance and a story in the *Modesto Bee* that concluded, "No one knows for sure who took the bell or where it is now."

The sisters offered to pay $200 toward the $1,000 cost of a new bell, but the school district rejected that offer. Meanwhile, amid the controversy, plans for a plaque that would have dedicated the new school building to Prothero were dropped.

A new 205-pound bell (a larger replica of the 125-pound brass original) was commissioned and donated by the children of Jack and Annie Nicolini in memory of their parents to be mounted in the pagoda atop the new school. And tempers must have eventually cooled, because the school named its all-purpose sports field Prothero Field in 1989, a year before the former teacher's death.

The bar inside the Chinese Camp Store. *Author photo*

What's in (the) Store

The Nicolini name is a prominent one in Chinese Camp, with John and Annie Nicolini having founded the Chinese Camp Store in 1934.

Then known as Nicolini's, the store still operates today. The Nicolinis operated it for some three decades, installing three motel cabins to go with the gas pumps out front and the bar inside—which functioned as an informal town hall. They both passed away in the mid-1960s, but not before leaving their mark on the community.

In addition to running the store, John Nicolini took it upon himself to renovate the old Catholic Church on the hill, which hadn't been used since the late 1920s. By the time he undertook the project in 1949, the church had fallen into a severe state of disrepair.

John and Dottie O'Brien bought the store around 1973. They'd vacationed in Tuolumne County for 17 years before they took the plunge and bought the place from Rose Pardini, John and Annie Nicolini's daughter. Their kids were all grown, so they decided to exchange life in Los Angeles for a slower pace in the Gold Country.

"We figured business would be slow and we could go fishing whenever we wanted," John O'Brien told *The Modesto Bee* in 1975:

It didn't work out that way.

"I've only been fishing once in three years," Dottie added. "The only fishing I do is out front" from the minnow tanks."

John took the reins as chief of the town's volunteer fire department, formed in mid-1974, further reducing his free time, and the store itself opened at 7:30 a.m. and stayed open until 11 p.m. on weekdays and 2 in the morning on weekends during summer.

Tourists might pop in anytime, but the town folk tended to stop by after 4 o'clock, he said. Then there were the town's 32 schoolkids, who showed up at lunch and after school to buy candy. The store was really hopping in the afternoons, with kids clamoring for sweet treats, locals sidling up to the bar, and travelers pulling up to one of the store's three gas pumps.

The O'Briens hightailed it out of town on Wednesday, thereby killing two birds with one stone. The only products sellers would deliver were bread and beer, so they had to travel to Modesto—about an hour west—to restock on everything else. They had to leave someone else in charge, but that was fine with them because, John said, "everybody who's mad at us comes in on

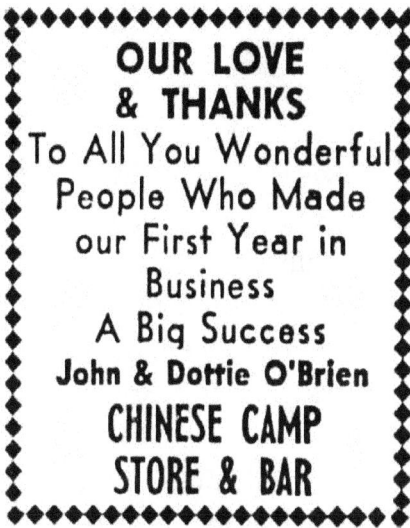

OUR LOVE & THANKS
To All You Wonderful People Who Made our First Year in Business A Big Success
John & Dottie O'Brien
CHINESE CAMP STORE & BAR

Wednesday."

Michael Read bought the store from the O'Briens in 1987 and owned it for three decades before current owner Richard Beale bought it. The gas pumps have been removed, but the bar's still open, the store still sells candy, and country music blares from the outdoor speakers, welcoming tourists, bikers, and other customers. There's a nice garden off to one side, with goats, a cat, and other critters wandering about. You can sit out there at one of the picnic tables or visit the restroom.

But other things have changed since the Nicolinis and O'Briens owned the place. The church that John Nicolini lovingly restored has, sadly, fallen into disrepair once again. Nicolini is buried in its graveyard.

And no one lives in the old Oddfellows Hall today. Even after being gutted by the 6-5 fire, it remains the tallest building in town, its stone walls standing resolute against an onslaught of overgrowth from trees of heaven. Inside, it's dark and deserted, sealed off from the world by "private property" signs and rotting wood—the white paint on the latticework peeling inexorably away.

Around 2013, a Modesto contractor named Frank Stanley and his wife, an interior decorator, announced plans for a $3 million project to transform the old Stratton place into a bed-and-breakfast. They planned to renovate the old post office across the street to serve as a visitor's center and museum.

The old Fox Boarding House would be transformed into a youth hostel, and the two-story Morris building would be used for retail space and lodging. Solinsky Alley was transformed into a garden-like setting in preparation, but unfortunately, the deal fell through and the plans came to naught.

In 2024, before the fire, Solinsky Alley was overgrown with weeds and traversable only by a gravel path. The rest of the buildings remained in a state of continued decay.

A Tour of Main Street

Take a stroll down Main Street of Chinese Camp, and you're not likely to find it much different than a stroll through the cemetery. There's little traffic, save perhaps for those peacocks and the occasional vehicle making the rounds to ensure no one goes poking around beyond the "no trespassing" signs.

It *was* a cemetery of sorts, even before the fire: A graveyard for the buildings that remain, rickety boards creaking in the late-afternoon wind, roofs caved in, iron doors barred, once-sturdy brick walls crumbling and overgrown with the trees of heaven.

Rusted, bent, and broken fragments of yesteryear on Main Street in Chinese Camp. *Author photos*

If you've been to Virginia City, a more famous boomtown not all that far away in the neighboring state of Nevada, you've seen the wood-plank walkways that line the streets. These were once here, too, and before they were incinerated, you could see what remained of them outside a couple of buildings on the south side of the road. Windows were broken, walls were riddled with holes, and one could only imagine how drafty the interior of these places could get. They might or might not have been haunted, but would you really want to spend the night inside one? "Private property" signs were enough of a deterrent without risking the wrath of the not-so-dearly departed.

What was still here in 2024, and what was long gone along this single block at the heart of a once-thriving town? Here are some clues to help you get your bearings.

This historical marker stands at the corner of Main Street and Highway 49. *Author photo*

The former IOOF Hall (Mountain Brow Lodge #82) stands at 10009 Main Street, on the southwest corner of Main and Highway 49— former Yosemite Avenue. Built around 1863, it's the only masonry structure in town. It also served as a meeting place for the Masons and Knights of Pythias before Dr. Daniel Stratton bought it and turned it into his family's personal residence, using some materials from Saul and Minnie Morris' old home, which had stood on the north side of Main Street west of Red Hill Road. *Author photo*

Above: The IOOF Hall is recognizable at left in this historical photo. At the center is the Eagles Hall, which was built as an annex for the Garrett House (far right) before later serving as a dance hall and community center. *Tuolumne County Historical Society*

Below: Solinsky Alley, runs between Main and Washington streets, next to the vacant lot once occupied by Garrett House. *Author photo*

Author photo

US POST OFFICE

Tuolumne County Historical Society

Across the street from the IOOF Hall stands this red-brick structure built in the 1850s as the Joseph Cohn Store. It's seen here in 2024 (top), and directly above when it was still serving as the post office. Later owned by the Morris family from 1862 to 1865 and the Morris brothers from 1891 to 1920, it was also the site of the post office, telephone office, and the last of four Wells Fargo locations in town. From 1872 to 1875, the store was owned by Timothy McAdams.

Above: The photo above, dated 1930, shows what appears to be a continuation of the post office building, seen at right, that no longer exists. Attached and built in the same style, it has a separate front overhang and distinctive gable. *University of Southern California Libraries and California Historical Society*

Below: looking west on Main Street from Highway 49. *Author photo*

These two buildings, both visible from Highway 49, stood to the rear of structures on the north side of Main Street. The barn at top was built around 1900 and may have been a blacksmith shop at one time. The small stone outbuilding at right was behind the old post office and dates from the 1850s, having probably served as an outbuilding for the Cohn-Morris store. The area was decimated by the 2025 blaze.
Author photos

This brick wall stands on the south side of Main Street, just west of Solinsky Alley. The old Masonic Hall stood on this site, with the Fred Weyer Brewery immediately to the west. The tin storage building adjacent to the wall dates from the 1950s. The wall, which survived the 2025 fire, is seen at top from Main Street and directly above from behind on Solinsky Alley in 2024. *Author photos*

Photo courtesy of Richard Beale, Chinese Camp Store.

Grand Celebration

I.O.O.F.

THE FIFTY-FIRST ANNIVERSARY
ed in of the order in the United States, will be celebrat-

Chinese Camp,
— ON —

TUESDAY, April 26th, 1870.

A PROCESSION WILL BE FORM-
ed at 10 o'clock A. M., at ODD FELLOWS
Hall, which will proceed to the Garett House Hall where an ORA-
TION will be delivered;
the Celebration to close with

A Grand Ball
at the
GARETT HOUSE, CHINESE.

OFFICERS OF THE DAY.

PRESIDENT OF THE DAY,
E. MURDOCK, Esq.

ORATOR OF THE DAY,
JAS. LETFORD, Esq,

CHAPLAIN OF THE DAY,
Rev. J. M. Campbell.

MARSHAL OF THE DAY,
HENRY SCHULER, Esq.

COMMITTEE OF ARRANGEMENTS.

SONORA LODGE No. 10.
Daniel Sewell,   F. A. Freund,
                        TUOLUMNE LODGE No. 21.   W. W. Boyle.
A. B. Beauvais,   Ed. Parson,   G. Hudson.
                        MOUNT HOREB LODGE No. 38.
J. A. S. Trout,   E. Murdock,   A. Bullerdick.
                        YO SEMITE LODGE No. 97.
J. Sargent,   James J. Lounsion,
                        BALD MOUNTAIN ENCAMPMENT No. 4.   W. Hubbard.
C. H. Randall,   W. L. Sears,
                        KNIGHT'S FERRY LODGE No. —   I. J. Potter.
A. P. Battlett,   J. R. Horsley,   P. Englebart,
                        MOUNTAIN BROW LODGE No. 32.
George Hanna,   S. Pitman,   J. F. Sears,
J. K. Betts,   L. Mayet,   C. B. Cutting.

FLOOR MANAGERS.

S. M. Miller,
                        M. Bacon,   R. M. Lampson.

Music by Chinese Camp BRASS & STRING BAND,
J. K. Betts, Leader.

TICKETS,   (exclusive of Supper,) $2 00.
Chinese Camp, March 19, 1870 —6w

The Masonic Hall that stood across Solinsky Alley from the Garrett House featured a gabled roof and second-story balcony with an ornate railing. It was evidence of the active lodge community in town, as seen in the ad at right for a grand ball at Garrett House in 1870 celebrating the 25th anniversary of the IOOF.

The Elizabeth Fox Boarding House stood on the north side of Main Street, just west of a vacant lot that once housed Dr. Lampson's office. The building was moved to Chinese Camp after being originally constructed in Montezuma. It replaced the previous building on the site, the Miller and Solinsky express and banking building described in 1865 as a "one-story fireproof brick building with two safes and one pair of scales, and office fixtures."

Author photos

The New York Store, more popularly known as the Rosenbloom
Store (for owner Joseph Rosenbloom), is a shell of its former self.
The iron doors still stand firm, but the side walls and ceiling have
collapsed, as seen below in a view toward the intact but crumbling
back wall. Older photos show a gabled front. The building was
constructed in 1851, with the brick front added in 1854. Later, it
had gas pumps out front. A livery stable once stood to the west in
what is now a vacant lot. *Author photos*

This building stood at the northeast corner of Main Street and Red Hill Road (Webster Avenue). Built around 1870, it was known as Gross' Saloon for its proprietor at the time of its construction, A. or C. Gross. An ad from October of that year, at right, indicates it was an official stop on the Peoples' Accommodation

PEOPLES' ACCOMMODATION STAGE AND EXPRESS COMPANY'S

STAGES LEAVE COLUMBIA, AT 2 o'clock, A. M., for STOCKTON, via Sonora, Jamestown, Montezuma, Chinese Camp, Crimea House and Knight's Ferry.

Leave Yo Semite House, at Stockton, at 6 o'clock A. M., and running each way on alternate days, connecting with Stages for Yo Semite at Chinese Camp and Crimea House. M. Kelly's Stages connect with the Stages at Sonora each day.

Office at Columbia	Gorham's Hotel
Office at Sonora	Sonora Hotel
Office at Jamestown	Bella Union Hotel
Office at Chinese Camp	Gross' Saloon
Office at Knight's Ferry	Washington Hotel
Office at Stockton	Yosemite & Weber Houses

Fare Through Reduced to $5.

ROBERT BOYD,
General Superintendent.

jun18-tf

Stage and Express Company's line. The line was doing a good business that year: "This week," it was reported in September, "the accommodation is not sufficient to carry all the passengers traveling on the line without putting on an extra." Samuel Wheelock, who operated a saloon across the street, had come into possession of the building by 1891, and Saul Morris owned it from 1901 to 1920. *Author photo*

The Robert Orford Store, on the south side of the street across from Rosenbloom's, was built in the 1850s and is sometimes called the "Fandango House." That establishment, however, was housed in a separate structure. Known as "Frank's Fandango House" for its owner, Frank V. Losano, it occupied an adjacent building (to the east, at the left in this photo) that no longer exists. Frank's was apparently one of at least three such businesses in town: combination drinking halls, dance parlors, cardrooms, and brothels. Its central position on Main Street likely made it the most popular. Orford, a merchant, operated a store in the 1850s structure on land owned by a man named Wolf. He owned the property through at least 1871, and an 1873 map marked the lot as belonging to "J. Morris, Agt." It later passed into the hands of Joseph Rosenbloom, proprietor of the New York Store across the street, who owned it for several years at the end of the 19th century. The lot west of the Orford Store once housed another mercantile, the Buck Store. *Author photo*

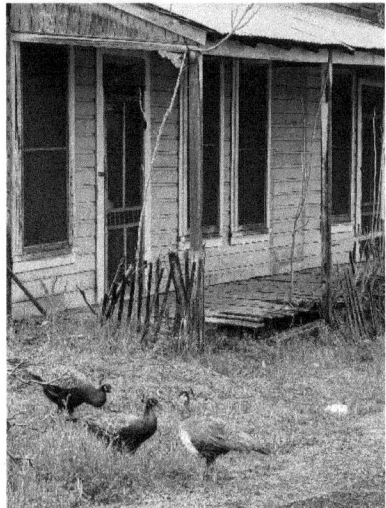

Another building sometimes confused with the Fandango House, this home or boarding house sits at the southeast corner of Main Street at Red Hill Road/Webster Avenue. The structure's layout as a duplex might have meant it was built to serve as rental housing for its owners, probably the Morris family. Constructed around 1890, it stood on property that, 17 years earlier, had been credited to someone in the Morris family on the town map. This would have made sense, because the Morrises at one time or another owned property on the other three corners of the intersection: The Walkerley Store across Webster Avenue, a warehouse on the northeast corner (with Saul Morris' home next door), and later on, the former Gross Saloon. *Author photos*

This grand home, which stood just west of the Main/Webster intersection on the north side of the street, belonged to Saul Morris. It no longer stands. According to a newspaper account, Morris sold it and had it divided into two pieces around 1920, which became separate residences in Oakdale. About the same time, Dr. Stratton's home at the other end of Main Street burned down, and Stratton apparently used some elements of the Morris house to adapt the IOOF Hall into a personal residence. The photo directly above shows the same house looking east on Main. The turret has been drawn in. *Courtesy of Richard Beale, Chinese Camp Store*

The Oddfellows Hall at Highway 49/120 and Main Street, later the Stratton residence, was left a shell of its former self. *Author photo*

The 2025 Fire

On September 2, 2025, a lightning-caused fire swept through Chinese Camp, destroying many of the historic buildings on Main Street and leaving a number of community residents homeless. The fire, which burned nearly 7,000 acres, spared the 1854 St. Francis Xavier Church and adjacent cemetery, along with the Chinese Camp Store, as well as modern buildings such as the new school, post office, and fire station. The town was evacuated, and some forty homes and seventy structures were lost.

The historic artifacts in Beale's collection, some of which are shown in this work, also survived undamaged.

Unfortunately, many of the buildings featured on the preceding pages were among the losses. Chinese Camp Store owner Richard Beale described it as like being next to a volcano: "All these burning embers were falling down. It was like being in

Pompeii." Main Street, Beale said, was "completely obliterated. There were seven or eight Gold Rush or Victorian-period buildings that were beautiful, that were our connection to the past, and they're just empty shells now. Elizabeth Fox's boarding house is just flat ground; it was all wood, so there's nothing left.

"The Stratton House is still there, but it's hollow, and it's beautiful in its own way. A few of the stone or brick walls are still there as a reminder; I hope a few of them stick around and don't get knocked down for safety reasons."

Following are photos taken Sept. 14, 2025, which show Main Street after the fire.

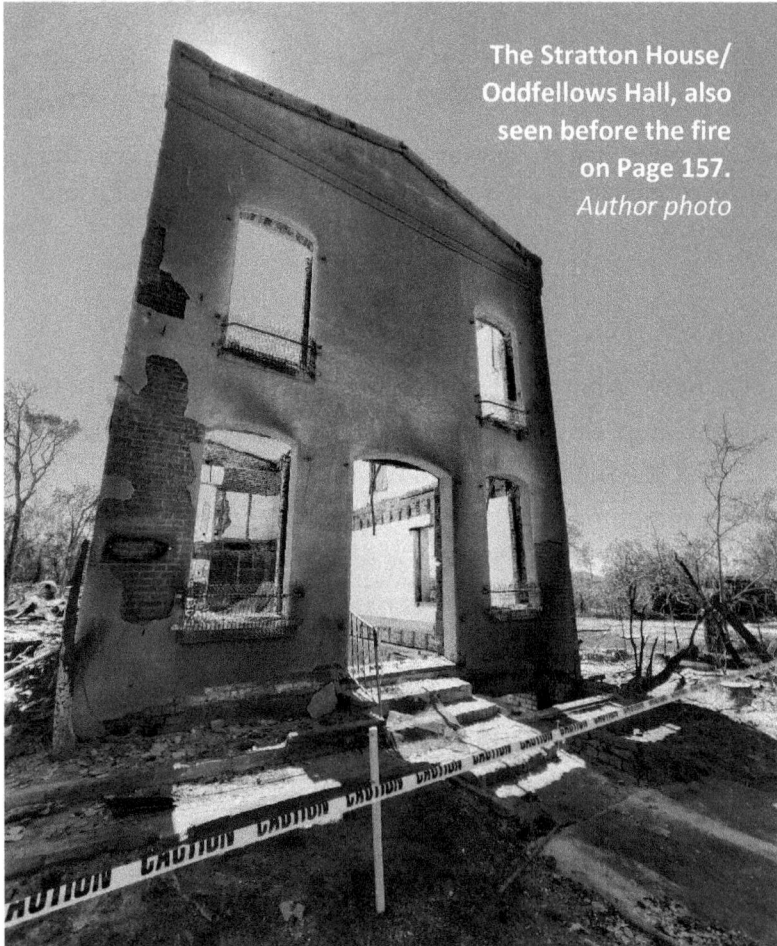

The Stratton House/ Oddfellows Hall, also seen before the fire on Page 157. *Author photo*

Top: Looking east on Main Street, with the vacant lot once occupied by the Fox Boarding House in the foreground and the Cohn-Morris Store/ Post Office next door.

Above: The view from Red Hill Road east on Main. The ruins of the New York Store can be seen at left, with the walls of the Robert Orford Store at right. The two lots in the foreground, now vacant save for strewn metal wreckage, belonged to the A. Gross Saloon (left) and two-story Morris home (right.)

From top: The old post office/Cohn Morris Store (page 159); the Fox Boarding House lot (page 164); and Solinsky Alley (page 158) after the fire. *Author photos*

The brick wall on the site of the old Masonic Lodge and brewery (page 162), with the Oddfellows Hall in the distance. *Author photo*

Chimneys are all that survive of the building adjacent to the old Oddfellows Hall. *Author photo*

Top: The Robert Orford Store, pictured on the cover and page 167, was reduced to a pair of brick walls and some junk inside.

Above: Front sections of brick wall and iron doors survived in the former New York Store/Rosenbloom Store (page 165) across Main street from the Orford Store. The left wall had already been lost, the roof caved in, and the back severely damaged before the fire. *Author photos*

Top: Twisted metal lies strewn across the site of the Morris Home at the southwest corner of Red Hill and Main Street. The building is shown intact on the back cover and on page 168.

Above: The now-vacant site of the A. Gross Saloon (page 166).
Author photos

STEPHEN H. PROVOST

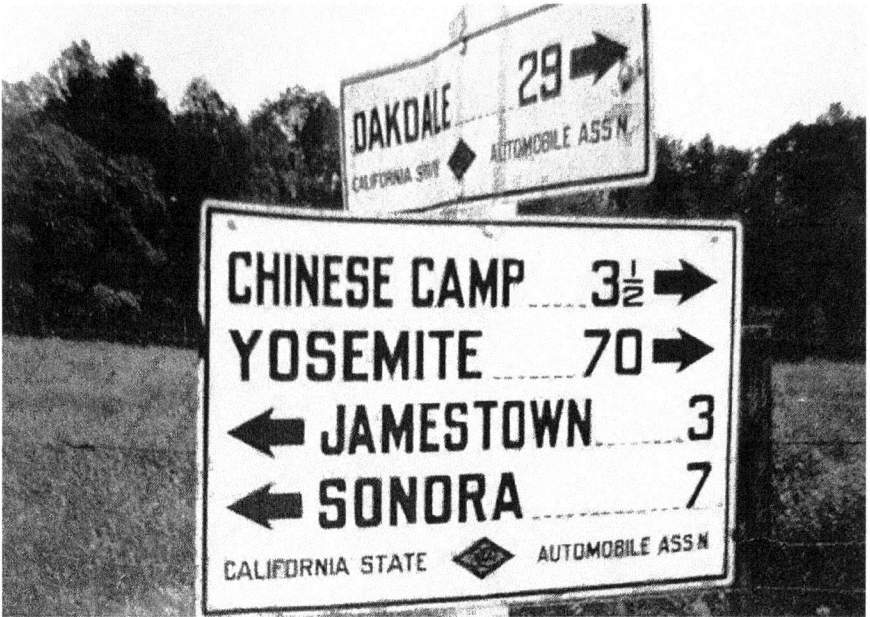

Old California State Automobile Association Sign, probably at the junction of State Routes 49 and 108, midway between Jamestown and Chinese Camp. *Photo courtesy of Joel Windmiller*

In the Neighborhood

Chinese Camp was one of many towns, camps, ranches, and mines in Tuolumne County that were bristling with life during the Gold Rush era. To be sure, it was one of the more prominent sites: During its history, prospectors extracted some $2.5 million worth of gold from the area.

Some spots that once graced the map are gone now. Others are just bends in the road where you might see a barn or an old home, but little else. Still others continue on as towns or hamlets with varying degrees of activity.

Here are just a few of the places near Chinese Camp that played a role in its history and the history of the region as a whole.

Algerine

An old home and bar along Algerine Road. *Author photo*

Today just a collection of scattered ranches and a few barns, Algerine Camp was founded in 1853. Curtisville, which was mentioned as having a post office that same year, was just two miles away. In its heyday after the discovery of gold there, the community consisted of a wide street and buildings that included a hotel, and as many as 20 frame houses along with numerous miners' tents.

About 11 miles northeast of Chinese Camp via Highway 49 to Jamestown, then south on Algerine Road.

Big Oak Flat/Groveland

The Big Oak for which Big Oak Flat is named no longer stands. *Library of Congress*

On the way to Yosemite past Priest Grade and the summit, this town was once known as First Garrote. (There was also a Second Garrote a little farther east on the road.) Garrotes were hanging trees, so named for the Spanish word for choking, and First Garrote was named as the result of an incident in 1849 after a couple of men robbed an adobe trading post there of $200 in gold dust... and were strung up for their crime. Big Oak Flat just sounded better. The Big Oak in question was big indeed, but it's no longer there (apart from some remnants contained in a historic roadside marker). The community had some 200 buildings by the 1860s, but many were destroyed by a fire in 1863. The IOOF and Wells Fargo buildings, which were made of stone, survive. Groveland, less than two miles farther to the east, is home to the 1852 Granite Store, now rechristened the Iron Door Saloon. The Garotte Post Office was changed to Groveland in the 1870s. The *Sonora Union Democrat* didn't appreciate the government changing the name, although it had to admit: "Garrote is not a very pretty name, and has unpleasant associations."

About 15 miles southeast of Chinese Camp along State Route 120.

Camp Salvado

Also known as Campo Salvado or Camp Salvador, this mining camp was about a mile east of Chinese Camp and was actually founded first. Chinese miners, unwelcome there, moved to the site that became Chinese Camp, which was called Washington Camp at that time. As time went by, the settlement was referred to by some as East Chinese. Nothing remains of Camp Salvado today, but it was once the site of a rough and rowdy saloon where the first sheriff of Amador County was killed by a fleeing fugitive.

About a mile east of Chinese Camp, formerly via Main Street past the church, but the road ends at St. Xavier's now, and what lies beyond is on private land.

Cloudman's

This ranch, a couple of miles west of Keystone, was named for Daniel Cloudman, who came to California from Maine in 1850 and started out as a miner. He opened a tavern for teamsters on the road between Chinese Camp and Knight's Ferry, halfway between the two towns, and also operated a hotel—but that burned down three days before Christmas in 1874. A post office opened at Cloudman's in 1882, by which time its original owner had sold the place to John Curtin. But Cloudman continued to live there, serving as postmaster. The post office was actually in Curtin's front room, and it was in that room that Tuolumne County's first toll phone was installed in 1895. The post office was discontinued in 1905 when the mail was transferred to the new Keystone Post Office nearby.

About 8 miles southwest of Chinese Camp.

Columbia

The St. Charles saloon stands at the northeast corner of Jackson and Main Streets. Martha's Saloon, which no longer stands, was at the southwest corner of the same intersection, where the California Store now stands. *Author photo*

As the Barclay lynching illustrates, Columbia was a rowdy place. And it's no wonder: Between 5,000 and 10,000 miners descended upon the camp in the early 1850s, making it one of the state's largest towns. The town had Chinese residents and businesses, though they weren't always welcome: In September of 1857, the town passed an ordinance "requiring the Chinese to leave town within a specified time" because it was supposedly "necessary for the safety of the place." Some doubtless headed south to Chinese Camp, but the ordinance wasn't exactly effective: By 1860, more than 30 Chinese businesses were operating in Columbia, including a brothel with 32 prostitutes.

This was far from unusual. In fact, some 3,500 Chinese women were living in California by 1870, with more than 2,100 working as prostitutes. By then, Chinese residents had moved into the old French district, where Sam Lun Sing was running The Old China Store in the former Claverie Building (constructed in 1857, its ruins can still be seen today). A joss house and Chinese theater were adjacent to the store.

With eight hotels and 40 saloons in town—Martha's was far from the only one—there was keen competition among madams, miners, and pretty much everyone else. That meant there were plenty of opportunities for fights to break out—especially with more than $150 million in ore recovered from the area in the decades after the initial strike. One such dispute resulted in the killing of a local man and brought none other than James Coffroth—the man later most responsible for Barclay's hanging—into the picture. Columbia was called "The Gem of the Southern Mines" and, at the time, in the midst of a heated competition with Sacramento over which city would become the permanent state capital. According to Coffroth's biography, petitioners had gathered some 10,000 signatures in Columbia's favor and placed them in a vault for safekeeping. Coffroth, a lawyer working on the accused behalf, somehow gained access to the vault and severed the signatures from the petition. He then attached them to a new petition seeking clemency for the killer, which he sent to the governor—who granted it. The accused killer was absolved, and Columbia lost out on its chance to become the capital of the Golden State.

About 13 miles north of Chinese Camp via State Route 49, a couple of miles east of the highway.

Goodwin's

Today known as Yosemite Junction, Goodwin's was a waystation where state routes 108 and 120 intersect. J.W. Goodwin founded the place in 1854 and ran it for the next 27 years, building a winery on his ranch. It was once marked by a road sign on a large block of wood hanging from a tree. The sign showed a pigtailed Chinese worker wearing a pack and included the words: "Me go China Camp... Three mile one half."

Less than 4 miles northwest of Chinese Camp via State Route 120 at the 108 junction.

Above: Old buildings sit abandoned at Yosemite Junction, above, but they date from the 20th century.

Left: An old stone fence across the street. *Author photos*

Green Springs

This 1914 bridge at Green Springs sits a little south of the Crimea House site. *Author photo*

Green Springs stood north of the Sonora Road (Highway 120) just over half a mile from the turnoff to Keystone. Named for two springs surrounded by thick tangles of blackberry vines, it was the site of another early post office, which is explicitly referenced in Bret Harte's story *A Sappho of Green Springs*. Harte's tale includes instructions from a poet to an editor to "send the money to Lock Box 47, Green Springs, P.O., per Wells Fargo's Express." The story also refers to a Green Springs Hotel.

About 6 miles southwest of Chinese Camp via Red Hill and La Grange roads.

Jacksonville

Jacksonville, with Richfield station, before it was submerged by Lake Don Pedro. *Photo courtesy of Richard Beale, Chinese Camp*

Jacksonville was founded in early 1849 by Col. A.M. Jackson, who built a mercantile there after finding gold on Sullivan's Creek at its confluence with the Tuolumne River. The location was also the site of the first orchard in Tuolumne County, planted by a man named Julian Smart (who actually got there before Jackson) and subsequently known as Spring Garden. By 1850, it was the county's second-largest town, and a post office opened a year or two later. The Jacksonville Damming Co. organized in 1850, dug a canal to divert the Tuolumne River and built a wing dam that allowed them to extract $16,000 worth of ore in just 15 days. Between $9 million and $40 million worth of gold was discovered there. But, ironically, the entire townsite was submerged in the late 1960s by another dam, which expanded Lake Don Pedro.

About 7 miles southeast of Chinese Camp on Highway 49, commemorated by a historical marker.

Jacksonville c. 1930, from top: A blacksmith's sign; looking up the road at Table Mountain; shacks along a dirt road. *University of Southern California Libraries and California Historical Society*

Jamestown

Jamestown depot on the Sierra Railway. *Author photo*

Tuolumne County gold fever started just south of Jamestown at Woods Crossing, named for the man who first discovered gold there. A whopping 75-pound nugget was pulled from Woods Creek, and the rush was on. Jamestown itself was named for Col. George James, who established a trading post and reportedly plied miners with champagne to have the town named after him. But when he hightailed it out of town under cover of darkness without paying these same miners, they renamed the community American Camp. The name didn't stick, though, because most folks kept calling it Jamestown (or "Jimtown"). It was formally changed back in 1851. Just before the turn of the century, in 1897, the completion of the 75-mile Sierra Railway steam train line was celebrated in Jamestown. A state park and museum there preserve its buildings and artifacts. The town has also hosted film crews for such TV productions as *Green Acres*, *Little House on the Prairie* (scenes were also shot at Knights Ferry, below), along with movies like *High Noon* and *Back to the Future III*.

About 6.5 miles north of Chinese Camp on Highway 49.

Keystone

Keystone was a crossroads community on the old Sonora Road, which looped down just south of the current Route 120 at its junction with La Grange Road. William H. Field built the Keystone House there in 1870, giving the place its name. A post office was established at Keystone on the Sierra Railway line in 1905, but the mail was transferred to Chinese Camp in 1913.

About 6 miles southwest of Chinese Camp via Red Hill Road and La Grange Road.

Knights Ferry

There's no ferry across the Stanislaus River at Knights Ferry, and there hasn't been for a very long time. But ferries were once the best way to cross big rivers, and others such as Parrott's Ferry and O'Byrne's Ferry operated across the same river. The ferry was replaced by a bridge, built to serve David Locke's flour mill, in 1857. But that bridge was destroyed five years later in a major flood. The present covered bridge, the longest west of the Mississippi, was built to replace it, with Chinese Camp wagon-builder and blacksmith Louis Egling playing a key role. The initial ferry, however, was the brainchild of William Knight, a physician and fur trader who had visited the area as a guide with John C. Fremont's expedition in 1844. After the discovery of gold, he set up the ferry in 1848 as a way to access the Southern Mines. It proved a gold mine in the figurative sense, earning him a whopping $500 a day. But his success may have made him a target, because he was gunned down at the center of town in 1849 by an assailant whose name has been lost to history.

About 18 miles west of Chinese Camp, just north of State Route 120.

Above: Chinese Camp blacksmith and wagon-builder Louis Egling received the contract to build the iron truss rods for the Knights Ferry covered bridge over the Stanislaus River. At 330 feet in length, it is the longest west of the Mississippi.

Right: The grist mill adjacent to the bridge, built in 1854.
Author photos

Moccasin

A company town dating from the early 1920s, Moccasin was built to house workers constructing the Moccasin Powerhouse. The original powerhouse was completed in 1925 but stopped operating in 1969 when a new powerhouse replaced it. The town has no services or stores and is owned almost entirely by the City and County of San Francisco. It's not far from the mining town of Jacksonville, which was submerged by Lake Don Pedro when the old Don Pedro Dam was finished around the same time. The lake is named for Don Pedro Sainsevain, an early prospector who discovered gold at Don Pedro's Bar in 1848. The lake also submerged the nearby community of Steven's Bar, founded in 1849 and the site of the first bridge across the Upper Tuolumne River in 1857.

About 9 miles southeast of Chinese Camp on State Route 49/120.

Montezuma

Founded as a mercantile called the Montezuma House or Montezuma Tent by Sol Miller and Peter K. Aurand in May of 1850, prospecting began in earnest there two years later after a ditch and flume were built to facilitate placer mining. The population at that point was some 800 people, and the town included two hotels, four saloons, a post office, church, and an Adams Express office. The town was largely consumed by a fire that started at Clark's Hotel on June 29, 1866. The Fox Boarding House, built in Montezuma, was later moved to Chinese Camp, where it still stands.

About 4 miles north of Chinese Camp on Highway 49.

Poverty Hill

The Poverty Hill schoolhouse in Stent was built in 1857 and retains the community's former name. *Author photo*

This small community, now known as Stent, is on the other side of Woods Creek from Chinese Camp. The town was destroyed by a fire in 1854 but endured and, in 1895 was renamed Stent when a new post office was established there. The new name honored a local mine operator, Ernest Albert Stent, presumably because it lacked the negative connotations of the original name. (Oldtimers didn't like the change, but the younger generation prevailed.) But the school, though no longer hosting classes, is still called the Poverty Hill School. It dates to 1857 and retains the name by which the town was known back then.

About 8 miles from Chinese Camp via Highway 49 and the Jacksonville Road.

Priest Hill

W.C. Priest and his wife built a hotel at the summit of Priest Grade where stage passengers spent the first night after leaving Milton. W.C. Priest was the superintendent of the Great Sierra Stage Company and the force behind construction of the Big Oak Flat Toll Road: He pushed the franchise grant for the road through the California legislature. Priest's wife was known for operating the hotel and giving its guests a warm welcome. "She always greeted them with a glad hand and a merry smile," Chinese Camp pioneer Paul Morris recalled. "Her meals as well as her beds were the best."

About 13 miles southeast of town via Highway 120.

Shaw's Flat

Founded in 1850, Shaw's Flat was named for Mandeville Shaw, who had planted an orchard on the slope of Table Mountain a year earlier. Shaw's Flat was bustling with prospectors by 1851, when it boasted a population in the thousands and had poured $100,000 into the construction of permanent buildings: mercantiles, boarding houses, saloons, a bakery, and a printing office. The Mississippi House, built in 1850, was a hotel, stagecoach stop, saloon, and store, also housing the local post office. The town's most famous prospector was James G. Fair, who went on to become a U.S. senator and for whom San Francisco's Fairmont Hotel was named. He made his fortune as one of the Comstock's "Silver Kings" in Nevada after coming up empty in the Mother Lode.

About 11 miles north of Chinese Camp via Highway 49 on Jamestown Road.

Sonora

The Bradford Building, above, and Chinatown marker in Sonora.
Author photos

Mexican miners founded Sonora and named it in honor of their home state south of the border. Chinese prospectors flocked to the camp as well, but many left (a large number settling in Chinese Camp) to avoid persecution and the foreign miners tax. Still, there were 400 people of Chinese descent living there in the 1870s, with an active Chinatown district on a block bordered by Stewart, Lyons, Bradford, and Shepherd streets. Known as "The Queen of the Southern Mines," the town officially became a city in 1851 and remains the only incorporated community in Tuolumne County. It's also the county seat.

About 10 miles north of Chinese Camp via Highway 49.

Timeline

1849

Count Solinsky and Solomon Miller, future business partners, arrive in California separately, both from Pennsylvania.

1850

The Walkerley Brothers open a general store in Chinese Camp.

May — Sol Miller founds a mercantile with P.K. Aurand called the Montezuma House at Montezuma.

June 1 — California's new Foreign Miners' Tax of $20 a month takes effect.

June 19 — Robbers kill P.K. Aurand and leave Sol Miller critically wounded in a holdup; Miller would recover and form a partnership later that year with Count Solinsky as stage agents and businessmen that continues for the next two decades.

September — Reynolds and Company Express begins service from Sonora to the Southern Mines; Todd & Company begins service to the Southern Mines that same year.

Sept. 17 — Miners organize a form of self-government in Chinese Camp, setting rules for claim sizes, and electing an alcalde and sheriff.

1851

C.W. Culbertson, a native of Salem, Massachusetts who would

196

later become a prominent public official and vintner in Tuolumne, begins mining at Chinese Camp and lives there for five years before relocating to Moccasin Creek.

James Wallace Kerrick arrives in Chinese Camp, where he spends some time prospecting before returning to his native Kentucky; he would be back with his entire family in 1853.

The first Chinese child is born in Chinese Camp.

1852

James Morris establishes a store in Chinese Camp.

A boarding house for miners is founded in Chinese Camp, which would later serve as a church before being converted into the community school.

Louis Egling founds his blacksmith and wheelwright shop in Chinese Camp.

January — Three Mexican outlaws attack miners at Yaqui Camp near present-day Calaveritas; it's the beginning of a string of robberies attributed to Joaquin Murrieta and his cohorts, many of them targeting Chinese miners.

1853

J.W. Kerrick founds the Kentucky House, later called the Crimea House, at the junction of Mound Springs Road (now Red Hill Road) and La Grange Road; in Chinese Camp, the Garrett House and Eagle Hotel are founded.

A gold nugget is found near Montezuma weighing 18 pounds, 8

ounces.

Feb. 25 — Two hundred Chinese miners arrive in the Southern
Mines.

1854

Alexander Stair moves from Mariposa County to Chinese Camp;
he serves as a stage agent there for the next nine years.

J.W. Goodwin builds a waystation for travelers at Yosemite
Junction, near the present intersection of state routes 108 and 120.

April 18 — The Chinese Camp Post Office opens.

1855

William A. Phoenix, the first sheriff of Amador County, tracks a
fugitive to Reitz's Saloon, about a mile east of Chinese Camp; the
sheriff is killed in the struggle that ensues, after which the wanted
man is captured and hanged from an oak tree.

St. Xavier's Catholic Church opens its doors on a hill overlooking
Chinese Camp, with Father Aleric presiding over a congregation
of 30 members

Oct. 10 — Chinese Camp pioneer John Barclay is hanged by a
mob in Columbia after fatally shooting John H. Smith at Martha's
Saloon. there. One of the biggest memorial services in the young
county's history is later held at the new St. Xavier's.

1856

The Robert Orford Store is built on the south side of Main Street in Chinese Camp.

June 8 — Fire races through town, causing $74,000 in damage and destroying much of Main Street. Miller and Solinsky's Pacific Express Office and the fireproof Vedder & Cutler building survive, but buildings like the Eagle Hotel and Garrett House are among 33 structures damaged.

Sept. 26 — The Sam Yap and Yang Wo groups assemble near Crimea House for what is commemorated as the first Tong war in California; it costs some $60,000, involves thousands of combatants, and leaves four men dead... all over a dispute regarding a single rock.

Sept. 30 — Two men are burned to death at the Belvidere House near Chinese Camp.

Nov. 1 — Two robbers separate some Chinese Miners of $40 in coins near Kentucky House, which is sold that same year to new owners and renamed the Crimea House.

1857

Jan. 29 —Several Chinese miners are working a plot of ground they'd purchased near Chinese Camp when a group of Americans confronts them, seizing their property. A struggle ensues, and five of the Chinese suffer fractured skulls; three are very critically injured.

1862

A flood destroys the first bridge at Knight's Ferry.

James Morris moves his business to Main Street into a building now known as the Cohn-Morris store; it stands near the intersection of Main Street and Highway 49 and long housed the post office.

April 26 — California passes the Anti-Coolie Act, designed to discourage Chinese immigrants from competition with "free white-labor." The act imposes a $2.50 monthly tax on members of the "Mongolian races" who weren't paying the Foreign Miners Tax or engaged in specified forms of agriculture. Businesses that hire Asian workers must pay the tax.

May 26 — A Chinese immigrant stabs and kills another man from China, and upon being jailed for the crime, hangs himself in the cell.

Aug. 9 — Irish immigrant Andrew Hempfield, 31, is killed in a cave-in at Chinese Camp.

1863

Fire burns several buildings in Chinese Camp.

1864

A lynch mob in Chinese Camp takes two Mexican prisoners named Luis Leiva and Sosme Nunes, and hangs them from a nearby tree, preventing their scheduled delivery to the Sonora Jail the following day.

1866

July — The town of Montezuma is destroyed by fire. The fire, which started in Clark's Hotel, is initially blamed on a drunkard, but the proprietor and his wife are later arrested on charges of arson in Chinese Camp and released after posting $500 bail. They are accused of setting the fire for the insurance payout.

1867

February — Daniel Cutting and his two-horse team perish in a flash flood at Six Bit Gulch.

1869

April — A woman named Mrs. Roessler is thrown from a buggy and killed near Chinese Camp.

April 22 — The Harris & Rodden store at Montezuma burns to the ground, causing an estimated loss of $8,000.

1870

R.M. Lampson sets up a medical practice and drugstore in Chinese Camp, having relocated from Montezuma.

Aug. 30 — Fire consumes the Chinatown district of Chinese Camp, causing a loss of $28,000.

1873

June 24 — A Chinese outlaw named Chang Wy resists arrest after being accused of attempted murder; he later commits suicide.

1875

Dec. 1 — A bandit holds up the Chinese Camp stage two miles from the Union Bridge across the Stanislaus River. The driver, who is alone in the stage, does not resist, and the outlaw makes off with $600.

July 8 — A fire at Chinese Camp causes an undetermined loss; insured losses amount to $9,000.

1876

May 15 — Fourteen-year-old John Wagner kills his brother Charles with an accidental shotgun blast at Chinese Camp.

1878

Feb. 2 — Fire destroys Dr. Lampson's office and drugstore in Chinese Camp; the loss is estimated at $3,000.

1880

Sept. 1 — A blaze destroys Louis Egling's blacksmith shop and also torches a lumberyard, along with barns owned by Michael Wilson and James Morris, and a lumberyard. Insured losses are placed at $3,800.

1881

The Tioga Mine Road into Yosemite is built, using largely Chinese workers.

1882

President Chester A. Arthur passes the Chinese Exclusion Act, a 10-year moratorium on any Chinese laborers coming into the United States.

Feb. 3 — The Chinese Camp stage is robbed of nearly $300, and a lawman named McQuade gives chase, but it's an express company detective who ultimately apprehends the bandits (two former convicts) in San Benito County. One of the men, Frank Rolfe, is sentenced to life in prison, while the other, Joseph Hampton, gets a five-year term.

1883

Sept. 4 — Tioga Road is completed.

1889

Oct. 10 — Dr. Daniel Stratton and Helen A. Cutting of Chinese Camp are married by the Rev. H.L. Gregory at Farmington in San Joaquin County.

1892

The Chinese Exclusion Act is extended for 10 more years.

1895

Nov. 8 — George Morris is fatally shot at the Wells Fargo office in Chinese Camp. Morris, the assistant postmaster and Wells Fargo agent, is the son of pioneer merchant James Morris and brother of merchants Paul and Saul Morris.

Dec. 2 — Wesley and Albert McReynolds are arrested in the murder of George Morris.

1897

Nov. 10 — The Sierra Railway line is completed, with several thousand people attending festivities to mark the event in Jamestown.

1899

May 1 — Daniel Lumsden of Chinese Camp purchases the Great Sierra Stage Company from Captain W.A. Nevillis. He would later continue to operate the stages under the auspices of the Morris Brothers.

1902

The Chinese Exclusion Act is made permanent.

1904

Supposed ghost sightings wreak havoc in Chinese Camp, with men stocking up on guns and ammo after several people report seeing a figure in a white mask peeking through windows, disturbing gardens, and walking around in town and at the Eagle-Shawmut Mine.

1906

Chinese Camp has a new schoolhouse on the hill opposite St. Xavier's.

Sept. 14 — Yet another fire torches Chinese Camp, damaging the Morris Brothers store, Masonic/Knights of Pythias Hall, the offices of Dr. Stratton, and a building owned by A.W. Bruigh containing hay, stages, and other vehicles.

1910

Viola Prothero begins a 47-year career teaching at the Chinese Camp School.

1914

Saul Morris ends stage service from Chinese Camp, advertises automobile service to Yosemite.

1916

Jan. 4 — Chinese Camp secures a place on the planned state highway with a decision to route the road from Jacksonville up the Eagle-Shawmut Grade through town and on "to the Goodwin place [Yosemite Junction]," where it would "connect with the Sonora lateral of the state highway." This more direct path is chosen over the option preferred by Jamestown, which would have routed the highway over the Jacksonville-Stent cutoff and had it join the Sonora lateral at Jamestown.

1920

Saul Morris has his house dismantled and moved to Oakdale in two pieces, where it becomes two cottages. He leaves Chinese Camp and relocates to Stockton.

1921

Sept. 16 — A fire wipes out most of the small community around Chinese Station, destroying two barns, a former saloon, and a bunkhouse—all owned by Henry Sims. Only the station itself and a freight shed remain intact.

1922

"China Sam" and "China Mary" return to their homeland, leaving Chinese camp without a single Chinese resident.

1934

John Sr. and Annie Nicolini open the Chinese Camp Store, then known as Nicolini's.

1949

John Nicolini Sr. funds the restoration of St. Xavier's Catholic Church.

The Crimea House is destroyed by fire.

1953

July — Saul Morris dies.

1963

June 25 — John Nicolini Sr. dies; his age is given in different obituaries variously as 70, 74, and 75.

1968

July 11 — Annie Nicolini dies at the age of 67.

1971

Students move into the new pagoda-style Chinese Camp school on 7.5 acres of land formerly owned by the Stratton family. The new site is acquired in trade for the old school and the land on which it is located.

1973

John and Dottie O'Brien purchase the Chinese Camp Store from the Nicolinis' daughter.

1974

March — Chinese Camp forms a volunteer fire department with a 25-year-old fire truck.

1990

January — Viola Prothero, longtime schoolteacher at Chinese Camp and daughter of Dr. Daniel Stratton and Helen Cutting, dies at age of 99.

2006

The old Chinese Camp schoolhouse, built in 1906, burns down.

2025

September — The 6-5 Fire destroys most of the historic structures on Main Street. The church and Chinese Camp Store are spared.

References

About Priest Station," prieststation.com.

"Anti-Coolie Act in 1862," foundationsoflawandsociety.wordpress.com, Dec. 12, 2016.

Baggelmann, Theodore. "5000 Natives of Orient Once Lived In Rich, Bustling Chinese Camp,"
    with photo of Rosenbloom store. The Sacramento Union, p. 13, Sept. 26, 1948.

Belezza, Robert A. "California Gold Country Explorer," Tour and Travel Media, 2022.

"Black Bart Had Rendezvous in This City Years Ago," Pomona Bulletin, sec. 2, p. 1, Aug. 27, 1922.

Bloomfield, Anne. "History of Chinese Camp," County of Tuolumne, 1994.

"Bridget Sims," findagrave.com.

"Brief Mention," Palo Alto Times Weekly, p. 3, May 28, 1897.

Buckbee, Edna Bryan. "The Saga of Old Tuolumne," The Press of the Pioineers, Inc., New York,
    1935.

"China Sam and China Mary Going Home After 65 Years," Stockton Record, p. 12, March 30, 1922.

"Chinamen Robbed," San Andreas Independent, p. 2, Nov. 1, 1856.

"Chinese Camp," bbbunny.com.

"Chinese Camp," Stockton Evening Mail, p. 7, Oct. 11, 1911.

"Chinese Camp Established In Early Days is One of Historic Mountain Places,"
    Fresno Morning Republican, p. 5C, March 9, 1924.

"Chinese Camp Home Destroyed by Fire," Stockton Record, p. 10, May 12, 1920.

"Chinese Camp, the Venerable Mining Town, is Now Terror-Ridden By the Queerest Ghost on
    Record," San Francisco Chronicle, p. 5, Sept. 18, 1904.

"Chinese Camp's 'Instant' Fire Unit," Modesto Bee, p. B-1, April 8, 1974.

"Chinese Is Almost Wiped Out By Fire," Oakdale Leader, p. 2, Sept. 21, 1921.

"The Chinese of Columbia, 1850-1963," columbiagazette.com.

"Coast Items," Los Angeles Evening Express, p. 2, Dec. 24, 1874.

"Coast News Clippings," Sacramento Union, p. 1, Sept. 11, 1880.

"Columbia, California - Gem of the Southern Mines," legendsofamerica.com.

"Conflagration at Chinese Camp," Jackson Weekly Ledger, p. 2, June 14, 1856.

"Crossing spans two centuries," Oakdale Leader, Events p. 1, March 3, 1982.

"Daniel C. Cloudman Dies at Hospital," Stanislaus County Weekly News, p. 3, Jan. 22, 1904.

Daughters of the American Revolution. "Vital records from the Daily Evening Bulletin, San Francisco,
    California, 1861," archive.org

DeLacy, Ron and Frank, Russell. "School honors teacher," Modesto Bee, p. B-2, Feb. 24, 1989.

Divoll, J.G. "A History of Tuolumne County," B.F. Alley, San Francisco, 1882.

"Drives in the Spike of Gold," San Francisco Call, p. 2, Nov. 11, 1897.

"Eagle-Shawmut Mine," goldexplorers.com, Nov. 9, 2014.

"An Extract: A Distinguished Author's Sketch of a Trip Through the Valley and Hills," Oakdale Graphic,
    p.1, March 7, 1888.

Fein, Julian. "Missing School Bell Tolls Only Bitterness," Modesto Bee, p. B-4, Aug. 7, 1971.

"Fight Between Americans and Chinese," Sacramento Bee, p. 2, Feb. 7, 1957.

"For Arson," Sacramento Bee, p. 3, July 23, 1866.

"From Stage Coach Pioneer," Oakland Tribune, p. 19, March 7, 1943.

CHINESE CAMP

"Full Account of the Chinese Battle," Empire County Argus, p. 2, Nov. 8, 1856.

Harte, Bret. "A Sappho of Green Springs," gutenberg.org.

"Hedges, Buck & Co.," Stockton Record, p. 1, April 22, 1897.

"History: The 1854 Tong War, California," feraljundi.com, Sept. 12, 2011.

Holland, John, "Restoring History," Modesto Bee, p. B1, June 10, 2013.

"Hutchings," Yosmite, nps.gov.

"I Knew Chinese Camp When—" Stockton Record, p. 9, May 27, 1938.

"In Tuolumne's Jail," San Francisco Call, p. 5, Dec. 3, 195.

"Incorporated – Articles of Incorporation," San Francisco Examiner, p 2, July 29, 1968.

"Information Wanted," Shasta Courier, p. 2, Oct. 8, 1854.

"James Wallace Kerrick Sr.," findagrave.com.

"Jamestown," Stockton Evening Mail, p. 7, Aug. 2, 1912.

"Jamestown and the Way West," tchistory.org.

"Jamestown, California," westernmininghistory.com.

Jenkins, Olaf P. "The Mother Lode Country: Geologic Guidebook Along Highway 49—Sierran Gold Belt," September 1948.

Johnson, Hall. "So We're Told: Tuolumne Pioneer," polishclubsf.org.

"Junk State Capitol to Save Murderer," Lodi News-Sentinel, p. 3, Aug. 10, 1938.

Kane, William D. "Legacy provides footnote," Modesto Bee, p. 4, Dec. 21, 1977.

"Killed to Glut a Girl's Vengeance," San Francisco Chronicle, p. 1, Dec. 2, 1895.

Knight, Martha Wheeler. "The Irish Whyte Brothers' Letters," Stanislaus Stepping Stones, Vol. 14, No. 1, static1.squarespace.com, Spring 1990

"Knight's Ferry, California," westernmininghistory.com.

"Knights Ferry," hiddenmesa.com.

Langley, Henry G. and Morrison, Samuel A. "State Register and Year Book of Facts, 1859," San Francisco.

"Letter from Chinese Camp," Sonora Union Democrat, p. 2, Aug. 30, 1856"Loney Family from County

"Local News," Sonora Union Democrat, p. 3, Sept. 24, 1870.

Longford, Ireland," loneyfamilylongford.wordpress.com, Aug. 21, 2015.

"Louis Egling," findagrave.com.

Love, Doug. "Knight's Ferry," retroramblings.nsgw.org, July 18, 2021.

"Lynch Law," Stanislaus County Weekly News, p. 3, Aug. 31, 1906.

"Martha Carlos: Information on a merchant," columbiagazette.com.

Morris, Paul. "Chinese Camp, Ghost Town, Had a Ghost," Stockton Record, Out-of-Doors Section, p. 1, Feb. 11, 1933.

Morris, Paul. "Destruction of Priests Brings Old Memories," Stockton Record, Out-of-Doors Section, p. 1, Aug. 21, 1926.

Morris, Paul. "Memories of Early Towns and Resorts on Big Oak Flat Road," Oakdale Leader, p. 1, Nov. 1, 1928.

Morris, Paul, "Robbery of Past Days Recalled," Oakdale Leader, p. 7, July 8, 1943.

Morris, Paul, "Tioga Road Owes Its Existence to Old Silver Mine," Fresno Bee, p. 19, July 26, 1925.

"Morris' Murderers," Oakdale Leader, p. 1, Dec. 6, 1895.

"Mountain Travel," Stockton Evening Mail, p. 3, May 26, 1888.

"Moving Chinese Camp Residence to Oakdale," Stockton Record, p. 9, July 21, 1920.

"Mrs. Stratton, Postal Family Member, Dies," The Modesto Bee, p. D-2, Feb. 17, 1965.

Nevada Journal, p. 1, April 6, 1855.

"One Bell, All's Well," Modesto Bee, p. B-1, Sept. 17, 1971.

Paden, Irene D. and Schlichtmann, Margaret E. "The Big Oak Flat Road," yosemite.ca.us, 1955.

Perry, Helen Carol and Lund, Helen Carol. "Chinese Camp's Dr. D.E. Stratton," Union Democrat, Dec. 3, 2020.

"Personal News of Five Counties: Chinese," Stockton Record, p. 10, June 23, 1919.

"A Pioneer's Death," San Francisco Chronicle, p. 9, April 6, 1896.

"Pioneers' Meeting," San Bernardino Daily Courier, p. 3, July 17, 1892.

"Post-Offices in Tuolumne County," Columbia Gazette, p. 4, Nov. 19, 1853.

"Quaint Chinese Camp Church and Its Cemetery 107-Year-Old Landmark," Stockton Record, p. 22, June 25, 1962.

"Recollections of Early Days by Eddie Webb, 81," Stockton Record, p. 28, May 9, 1961.

"Rites Held for Mrs. Hopkinson," Santa Rosa Republican, p. 3, March 7, 1932.

"Roadside History," Southern Tuolumne County Historical Society, grovelandmuseum.org.

Roberts, Paul Dale. "Biography," jazmaonline.boards.net.

Roberts, Paul Dale. "Haunted Chinese Camp," unexplained-mysteries.com, March 26, 2013.

"Saloons & Gambling Halls: 19th Century," columbiagazette.com.

"School Bell Disappears From Belfry," Modesto Bee, p. B-2, July 19, 1971.

Sheatsley, Tillie. "Three Generation Post Office Regime Ends in Chinese Camp," Stockton Record, p. 10, Feb. 23, 1967.

"A Short History of Sonora," sonoraca.com.

Sly, Judy. "It's a grocery… a bar… and it's a town hall too," Modesto Bee, p. A-13, Dec. 7, 1975.

Smith, Joe. "Ghost Of Miner Unjustly Hanged Still Haunts Old Chinese Camp," Fresno Bee, p. A-4, Dec. 17, 1950.

"Stagecoach Driver is Honored With Plaque in Chinese Camp," Stockton Record, p. 28, May 9, 1961.

"The Story of a Bowie," Stockton Evening Mail, p. 3, Feb. 10, 1888.

"Teaching Career Spans Period From Mine to 'Quiet Place,'" Stockton Record, p. 32, Sept. 4, 1958.

"Telegraphic Items From All Quarters," The Sacramento Bee, p. 3, Aug. 31, 1870.

"The Storm Etc.," The Sacramento Bee, p. 2, Feb. 23, 1867.

"Thrilling Tales of Early Days in Chinese Camp By a Pioneer," Stockton Record, p. B19, Nov. 8, 1919.

"To the Yo Semite," Stockton Evening Mail, p. 3, May 1, 1899.

"Tuolumne County, California," J.A. Van Harlingen & Co., Sonora, 1909.

"Tuolumne Leaders Hope for More Money From State to Finish Priest Grade Work," Stockton Record, p. 6, Dec. 18, 1926.

"Two Fires at Chinese Camp," Alameda Daily Argus, p. 1, Sept. 14, 1906.

"Use of Chloroform," Nevada Democrat, p. 2, Feb. 25, 1857.

"Valuable Mining Claims" ad, Columbia Gazette, p. 3, June 17, 1854.

"Via the Eagle Shawmut Grade," Stockton Record, p. 6, Jan. 4, 1916.

"Wagon days," Merced Sun-Star, p. 6, Aug. 3, 1992.

"Which Tunnel Was First Cut Is Not Certain," Stockton Record, Out-o-Doors Section, p. 1, Feb. 14, 1925.

Whipple-Haslam, Lee. "Early Days in California; Scenes and Events of the '50s as I Remember Them," Library of Congress.

Williams, Warren. "Chinese Camp," Modesto Bee, p. C1, Nov. 13, 1977.

"Wood Creek," The Nevada (California) Journal, p. 2, May 29, 1852.

"Young Florence Hutchings Was Yosemite's Legendary Lady," undiscovered-yosemite.com.

"Ziegler Hotel at Chinese Camp Burns to Ground," Stockton Record, p. 6, Aug. 15, 1917.

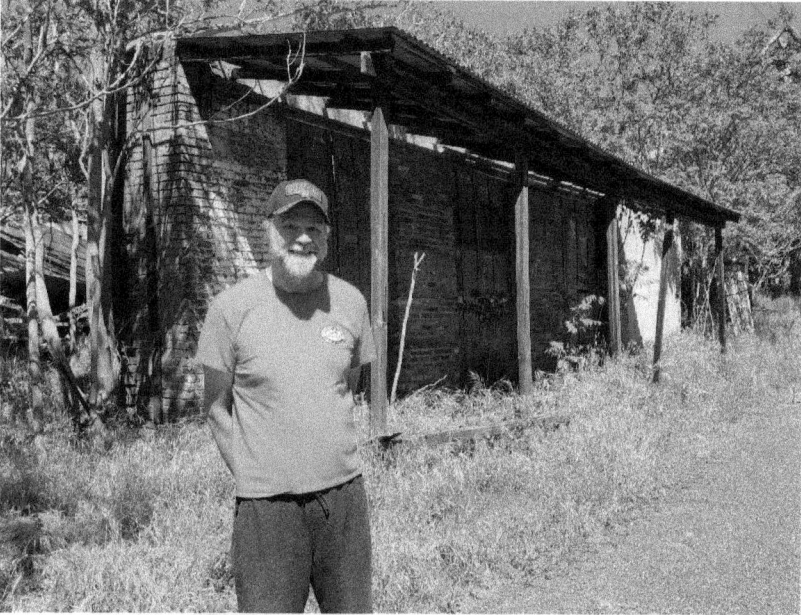

About the author

Stephen H. Provost is the author of numerous books on 20th century America, covering topics that range from his hometown to department stores and shopping centers; from pop music and sports icons to the history of our nation's highways. During a 30-year career in journalism, he worked as a managing editor, sports editor, copy desk chief, columnist and reporter at five newspapers. As a novelist, he has written about dragons, mutant superheroes, and things that go bump in the night. A California native, he now lives in Nevada. His books are available on Amazon or at dragoncrownbooks.com.

Did you enjoy this book?

Recommend it to a friend. And please consider rating it and/or leaving a brief review online at Amazon, Barnes & Noble andand Goodreads.

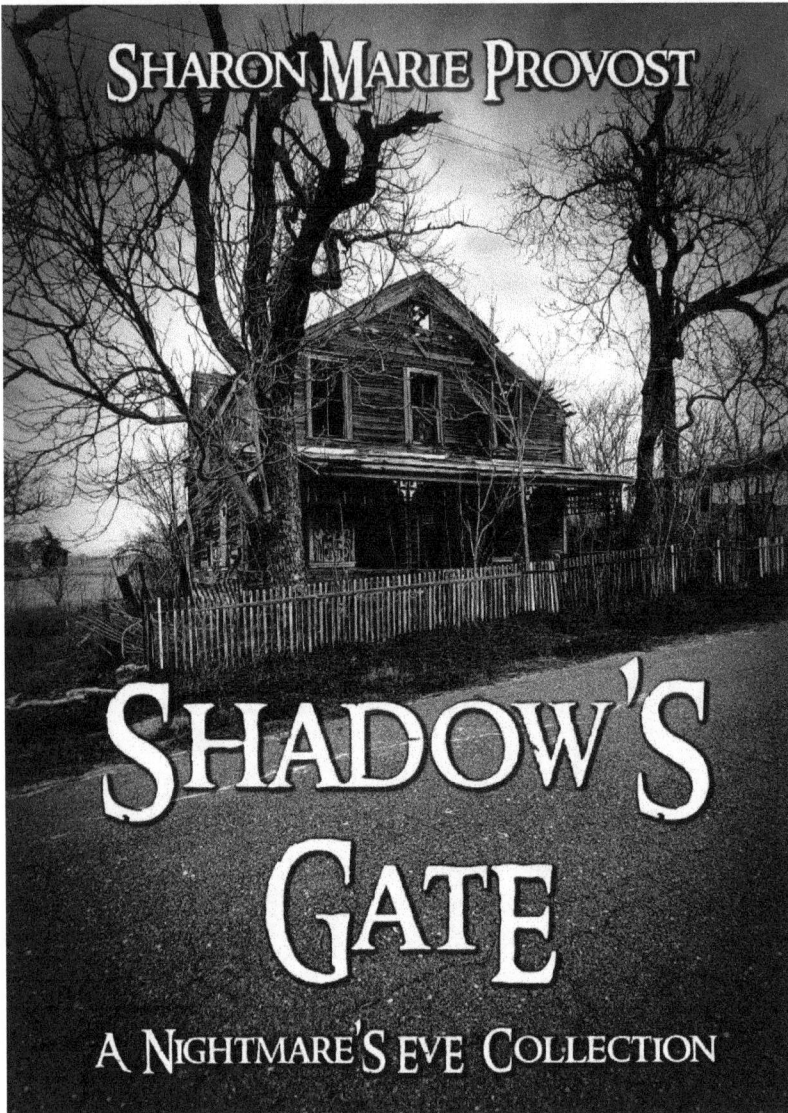

SHARON MARIE PROVOST

SHADOW'S GATE

A NIGHTMARE'S EVE COLLECTION

The Elizabeth Fox Boarding House in Chinese Camp is featured on the front cover of Sharon Marie Provost's collection of fictional horror stories, ***Shadow's Gate***. The first story is set in Solinsky Alley, which is depicted on the back cover. You can find Shadow's Gate on Amazon, at dragoncrownbooks.com, and at select retailers.

STEPHEN H. PROVOST

www.ingramcontent.com/pod-product-compliance
Lightning Source LLC
Chambersburg PA
CBHW052038090426
42739CB00010B/1964